"Not everyone will agree with Bose's prescription for a free society. However, in a decade when low birth rates and population collapse are gaining attention, expect more introspection like this. Bose argues that choices we have been taught to think of as private shape our economic future and even determine the survival of our civilization."
—JOY BUCHANAN, associate professor of economics, finance, and quantitative analysis, Samford University, Brock School of Business

"Bose's book is a tour de force on 'sexual freedom' in society. He builds on previous work about economic and political freedom, describing their relationship to well-being. He traces thoughts on sexual freedom by prominent thinkers and develops an 'index of sexual freedom' based on definitions of sex crimes and legal protections for marriage. The result is a provocative discussion of the relationship between prosperity and sexual restraint by individuals, society, and public policy."
—D. ERIC SCHANSBERG, professor of economics, Indiana University Southeast

"Dr. Feler Bose provides fascinating insight on an important, yet rarely discussed topic. He patiently and systematically offers resource data that creates a compelling argument that sexual freedom directly impacts economic progress. Utilizing pertinent case studies and historical expertise, Bose paints a moral landscape that serves as a cyclical harbinger of demise for future generations. Freedom, on any front, does not come without cost. Dr. Bose dares to ask the question, 'How much are we willing to pay?'"
—RICH HAWKINS, senior pastor, Christ Presbyterian Church, Richmond, Indiana

Sexual Freedom and Its Impact on Economic Growth and Prosperity

Sexual Freedom and Its Impact on Economic Growth and Prosperity

FELER BOSE

RESOURCE *Publications* · Eugene, Oregon

SEXUAL FREEDOM AND ITS IMPACT ON ECONOMIC GROWTH
AND PROSPERITY

Copyright © 2024 Feler Bose. All rights reserved. Except for brief quotations in critical publications or reviews, no part of this book may be reproduced in any manner without prior written permission from the publisher. Write: Permissions, Wipf and Stock Publishers, 199 W. 8th Ave., Suite 3, Eugene, OR 97401.

Resource Publications
An Imprint of Wipf and Stock Publishers
199 W. 8th Ave., Suite 3
Eugene, OR 97401

www.wipfandstock.com

PAPERBACK ISBN: 979-8-3852-0494-6
HARDCOVER ISBN: 979-8-3852-0495-3
EBOOK ISBN: 979-8-3852-0496-0

12/18/24

Contents

List of Table and Figures | vii

Preface | ix

Acknowledgments | xv

Biography | xvii

1. Sexual Freedom and Economic Freedom | 1
2. Micro and Macro Episode in the History of Sexual Freedom and its Impact | 20
3. History of Sexual Revolution in the U.S.: The Impact of Alfred Kinsey | 30
4. Assessing Sexual Freedom across the 50 States: 1960 to 2010 | FELER BOSE & ARI KORNELIS | 46
5. The Paths to Prosperity: Contemporary Theories on Global Wealth Accumulation | 67
6. Time Preferences and its link to Economic Freedom and Sexual Freedom | 86
7. Long-Term Thinking in the Bible and its Impact on Economic Growth and Prosperity | 102
8. Sexual Freedom, Guilt, Confession, and Its Impact on Economic growth and Prosperity | 126
9. Afterword | 141

CONTENTS

Appendix: From Sexual Freedom to Abortion Access and its Impact on the Future | BRIAN BAUGUS & FELER BOSE | 145

Bibliography | 165

List of Table and Figures

Table 1-1: Erotic representations over time based on 200,000 pictures and sculptures in Europe. | 16

Table 4-1: Variables used for developing the Sexual Freedom Index and the category of each variable. | 48

Table 4-2: Coding method used for creating the Sexual Freedom Indexes. | 53

Table A-1: Summary of Selected Studies of the Economics and Employment Impact of Abortion. | 156

Figure 1-1: Economic and Sexual Freedom Possibilities Matrix. | 15

Figure 4-1: Taking the total Sexual Freedom Index and subtracting the 2 variables showing the most variation shows that qualitatively the index doesn't change much. | 50

Figure 4-2: Lived freedom vs. median voter preferred Sexual Freedom Index. Three U.S. Supreme Court cases impact the Lived freedom index creating jumps in the Lived freedom index. | 59

Figure 4-3: Median voter preferred Sexual Freedom Index values from 1960 to 2010 going counter-clockwise from the top left. Darker shades indicate higher Sexual Freedom Index scores. | 62

Figure 4-4: Average state-level sexual freedom over 51 years. Hawaii on average has been the freest while Michigan is the least free. | 63

Figure 4-5: Marriage protection variables showing by their increase a decrease in the protection of sanctified marriage. Two of the variables show only minor changes. | 65

Figure 4-6: Four of the sex crime variables show a dramatic increase over the past 51 years. Rising tolerance for bestiality is reversed. Two of the variables show minor changes. | 66

Figure 5-1: History's hockey stick showing sustained economic growth starting with the United Kingdom. | 69

Figure 6-1: Two voter distributions on the time preferences spectrum and the impact on the median voter position. | 97

Preface

[T]he modern world with all its technologies, prosperity, justice, and knowledge, emerged [as the] result of the self-conscious decision of Christian men in many generations to forgo present consumption and invest in the future.[1]

BOJIDAR MARINOV

WHEN I STARTED MY Ph.D. program in economics at George Mason University (GMU), GMU had a vibrant economics department with a free market bent. I noticed that freedom in general was valued highly. Usually, this meant economic freedom, political freedom, and other personal liberties, including sexual freedom. Moreover, the literature on economic freedom is overwhelmingly seen as having positive impacts on various issues like prosperity (higher), corruption (lesser), human and social development (better), conflict (lesser), and so on. However, there was hardly any literature on the topic of sexual freedom. Dr. Peter Boettke, one of my professors at GMU always used to say we should do research that is not derived from the blackboard but by "looking out the window." That is, not to get caught up in what is currently fashionable among economists. He also encouraged us to be an earlier writer of a topic and not someone who is writing the 100th journal article on a topic, as our additional contribution to the topic would then be minor. This provided me with the impetus to work on this project further.

    1. Marinov, *Civilization and Self-Control*, 13th paragraph.

The issue of sexual freedom interested me as I noticed that the sexually free states in the U.S., were less free economically—this negative correlation needed further evaluation. Further, I did not see any literature on the topic of sexual freedom as a whole. However, there was a lot of literature on individual aspects of sexual freedom like divorce, homosexuality, abortion, etc. Is there a causal story for this negative correlation between economic and sexual freedom or is this by chance? It took me about four years after graduate school to start working on this project. While teaching at Alma College, I was fortunate to receive a semester-long research leave, which I spent at West Virginia University, a research-focused institution. The university's excellent law school and supportive staff assisted me in tracking sexual regulation laws across all 50 states. This collaboration enabled me to code the data and start conducting empirical analysis.

The Christian sexual ethic is clear starting from Genesis 2:24 where Adam is told to leave his parents and cleave to his wife, Eve. This precludes him from cleaving to multiple women simultaneously, cleaving to another man, cleaving to an animal, or cleaving to his family (incest prohibition). It also prohibits him from divorcing his wife. Further, in Genesis 1:27, God makes them Male and Female (binary by design, not a social construct). This sexual ethic is further elaborated later in Leviticus where we learn that certain sexual sins are seen as more serious and deserving of death because they are seen as treason to the family, whereas other sins are only fined. Sins such as polygamy were discouraged but if it occurred, it was regulated. In the New Testament, Jesus reiterates the commands from Genesis 1 and 2 (Matthew 19: 3–9) that divorce should be rare and not as common as the Pharisees had allowed for. In Romans 1:26, echoing Leviticus, homosexual sin is seen as a grievous one. Further sexual sin is a special type of sin that impacts the body and mind (Romans 1: 18–32, & I Corinthians 6:18–20). However, Paul also mentions that people who have committed sexual sins can find forgiveness in the work of Christ (I Corinthians 6: 9–11). The Christian message of love and holiness is to pray for sinners, call sinners to repentance by preaching the gospel, and that sinners cling to Christ.

Other religious faiths have various perspectives on sexual ethics. Most faiths have fewer sexual restrictions with some gods themselves being sexually promiscuous. For example, in Hinduism, some of the acts of Krishna such as when women come naked to him with hands lifted have sexual connotations, but some scholars have spiritualized it to mean that it is talking about the nakedness of the soul when coming before God. Many religious traditions also have dual and opposing perspectives on sexuality with some groups renouncing worldly pleasures for asceticism, and other groups being sexually libertine. For example, in Buddhism, monks were taught that sexual action and having children bring attachment and would hinder liberation. On the other hand, tantric Buddhism focused on cultivating 'sensual pleasures.' A few religions had similar sexual ethics as Christianity, they include smaller religions like Baha'i, Jainism, and Parsis with a focus on chastity before marriage and being faithful in marriage. In Islam, certain practices were dominant at times and not at other times such as *muta*. *Muta* is a temporary marriage where the man dictates a contract as to the length of the marriage. Money is exchanged during this period with the girl's parents. This marriage can last for a few minutes or many days. Critics of this arrangement consider it prostitution. It still occurs in some parts of the world. Further, under certain conditions, four wives were allowed, but unlimited concubines were permitted. Muhammed, the prophet himself had many wives though, he only took on additional wives after the passing of his first wife Khadija.[2]

In academia, the topics tied to individual sexual behavior have been written in countless peer-reviewed articles, books, law reviews, and so on. Depending on the subject area, the bias is generally pro-sexual freedom, that is, behavior outside of Genesis 2:24 is seen as good. Most trained economists writing in this area tend to be less biased as data analysis tends to drive their research; however, even that is subject to bias as pure neutrality is impossible.

2. Parrinder, *Sexual Morality in the World's Religions*, 5–262.

This book is not focused on the individual effects of people living outside the biblical framework of marriage and family. Numerous studies have shown the negative impact of living outside of marriage on children, the stability of marriages for those who cohabit or are sexually active before marriage, the impact of easy divorce laws, and so on.[3,4] Instead, this book will look at the broad effects of society not following the Biblical prescription for marriage and how it impacts civilization-building, as proxied by economic growth and development. Joseph Unwin, a scholar from the 1930s, argued that societies with sexual freedom tend to experience economic decline and eventual collapse, while those practicing sexual restraint become expansive and prosperous. I refer to this as Unwin's thesis. Why might this be the case? What aspects of sexual freedom lead to the downfall of societies?

This book is intended for an academically inclined lay audience from a Christian perspective. It can be used by advanced homeschoolers and in undergraduate courses at Christian colleges and universities. It will incorporate my academic work and contributions from numerous other scholars. The book will provide an economic foundation for Unwin's observations, demonstrating how societies that adopted strict monogamy standards built expansive civilizations.

Chapter 1 will explore how key thinkers have viewed sexual and economic freedom and their impact on prosperity. Chapter 5 will review economic research on various factors contributing to national prosperity, linking these findings to Unwin's assertion that sexual restraint positively influences economic growth and prosperity (Chapter 6). Additionally, the book will examine the relationship between economic and sexual freedom, and how these concepts connect with time preferences (Chapter 6). Chapter 7 will analyze Paul's instructions in the Bible advocating strict monogamy, particularly for men, and why these teachings and other biblical teachings are crucial for building an economically

---

3. Fagan and Churchill, *The Effect of Divorce on Children*, 1–48.

4. Stanley and Rhoades, *What's the Plan? Cohabitation, Engagement, and Divorce*, 1–37.

prosperous civilization. Given that sin leads to guilt, how does one address this guilt? Chapter 8 will delve into the effects of guilt from sexual sin on economic growth and prosperity.

Furthermore, Chapter 2 will review two historical episodes in which we observe what happens when sexual freedom changes and how it impacts society. Chapter 3 will explore the influence of Kinsey's research on the sexual revolution in the U.S., while Chapter 4 will codify the sexual revolution. Finally, the appendix will analyze the short-term and long-term effects of abortion, whose demand increases concomitantly with the sexual revolution.

Richmond, Indiana, USA

Acknowledgments

I would like to express my gratitude to Indiana University East, Richmond, Indiana, USA, for granting me a one-year research sabbatical, free from teaching obligations, to focus on this book project. Most of this book was written while I was volunteering at Kodaikanal International School (KIS), Kodaikanal, Tamil Nadu, India, in the academic year 2023–2024. I deeply appreciate the chance given by the KIS leadership to volunteer, the privilege for my family to reside in Kodaikanal, and the wonderful environment that facilitated my writing.

I would also like to thank Dr. Roger Congleton who invited me in the spring of 2012 to visit West Virginia University, Morgantown, West Virginia, USA. I was able to spend a lot of time at the law library there and begin my research work in earnest. I am also thankful for numerous students who worked with me on various aspects of this project over the years. Further, I am grateful for the numerous resource librarians who helped me over the years, especially Matt Dilworth from Indiana University East. I am also thankful to Dr. William L. Anderson whose economic insights early on into my work provided the impetus for further research.

I am grateful to Wipf & Stock Publishers for publishing this book. Further, this book was published with support from the Apgar Foundation which provided sabbatical funding and encouraged me to write for a broader audience rather than a strictly academic one.

ACKNOWLEDGMENTS

I am deeply grateful to my wife, Caroline, for her unwavering encouragement and support throughout the years, which has made this book possible. I am thankful to my parents for their major impact on my faith journey.

I dedicate this book to our four children, Theophilus, Luke, Makarios, and Mahila. They have made our lives a blessing, and they are a constant source of joy and gratitude.

Justice to Victory

Biography

DR. FELER BOSE IS an economics and finance professor at Indiana University East. His undergraduate studies culminated in degrees in Engineering Physics and Chemistry from Hope College, Holland, MI. He then completed his Master of Science in Mechanical Engineering from Georgia Institute of Technology, Atlanta, GA. He worked for a few years in the paper industry before realizing his interests were not in Engineering. He then returned to school and received his Ph.D. in Economics and a Master of Science in Economics from George Mason University, Fairfax, VA. He simultaneously completed his Master of Theological Studies from the American University of Biblical Studies, Decatur, GA.

Dr. Bose's research is multifaceted, encompassing applied microeconomics, political economy, law and economics, and the economics of religion. His current investigations delve into the impact of legislative structures on power dynamics, the significance of culture in societal development, and the opportunity cost associated with sexual freedom.

His scholarly contributions extend beyond academia. He has numerous publications in peer-reviewed journals and has authored book chapters, law briefs, and regulatory analyses. He has presented his research at several national and international outlets reaching a diverse audience of both professionals and lay audiences. He is a member of various professional organizations, and his outstanding contributions to teaching and research have earned him multiple awards at his current university.

BIOGRAPHY

Over his career, spanning the fields of Engineering and Economics, Dr. Bose has successfully secured grants of over a million dollars, underscoring his ability to combine academic insight with practical impact. His work continues to shape understanding in his fields of interest, inspiring students, researchers, and policymakers alike.

Deo Omnis **Gloria**

1

Sexual Freedom and Economic Freedom

As political and economic freedom diminishes, sexual freedom tends to compensatingly increase and the dictator... will do well to encourage that freedom. It will help to reconcile his subjects to the servitude which is their fate.[1]

ALDOUS HUXLEY, BRAVE NEW WORLD

AS STATED IN THE preface, most economists and academicians have an intuition that all freedoms are good, but observationally I find that in most cases there is an inverse relationship between economic freedom and sexual freedom. That is, when sexual freedom increases, economic freedom tends to decrease, and vice versa. In this chapter, I will first define economic and sexual freedom and how they tie in with prosperity. I also want to explore what other thinkers have said about the possible relationship between economic freedom and sexual freedom, though they might not use this exact terminology.

---

1. Huxley, *Brave New World*, 11.

WHAT IS ECONOMIC FREEDOM AND SEXUAL FREEDOM?

To achieve a high Economic Freedom of the World (EFW) rating, a country must secure private property rights, enforce contracts fairly and impartially, maintain a stable monetary environment, and allow freedom of international exchange. Additionally, the government should be minimal in size and regulation, keeping taxes low to encourage business development and investment. Avoiding unnecessary trade barriers and relying primarily on market mechanisms rather than government intervention for the allocation of goods and resources is also crucial. These combined elements foster economic predictability, growth, and a free and open market.[2]

Countries that have institutions and policies aligned with these principles of economic freedom, as measured by the EFW index, tend to perform better economically. They typically have higher per capita incomes, faster growth rates, lower poverty rates, higher rates of investment, and greater productivity per unit of investment. All these allow for the building of a prosperous civilization. These outcomes highlight the significant benefits of economic freedom.

In a similar vein, I propose a definition for minimum sexual freedom. This is when legal frameworks acknowledge only two individuals, a male and female, in a marital relationship as the only lawful sexual arrangement. This quantitative and qualitative recognition forms the basis for constructing a Sexual Freedom Index (SFI). This concept aligns with the teachings of Genesis 2:24. Historically in the United States, both family and criminal laws have advocated for confining sexual activities within the boundaries of marriage, as noted by Murray.[3]

---

2. https://www.fraserinstitute.org/studies/economic-freedom-of-the-world-2023-annual-report (accessed September 5, 2024).

3. Murray, *Strange Bedfellows: Criminal Law, Family Law and the Legal Construction of Intimate Life*, 1257.

When I first started working on this project many years ago, my initial hypothesis was that there is an inverse relationship between sexual and economic freedom in societies. This observation suggests that as societies become sexually free, their economic freedom tends to decrease. This perspective, however, is not universally accepted. Many of my academic peers believe that all forms of freedom, including political, personal, sexual, and economic, are interconnected and mutually beneficial.

Despite these differing viewpoints, there is a lack of empirical evidence to support either claim definitively. The Bible, however, offers some insight into this matter. It suggests that societies that defy God's Laws—including regarding sexuality—will face repercussions. These consequences often manifest themselves as economic hardships as indicated in Deuteronomy 28. Yet the underlying causal mechanism linking sexual freedom and economic freedom remains unclear. Why would these two forms of freedom move in opposite directions? This question calls for a deeper investigation and exploration that I will present in this book.

Before embarking on my research, I looked to see if there were existing studies or writings exploring the relationship between sexual and economic freedom by other scholars. I will explain some of the works by Adam Smith, Sigmund Freud, J.D. Unwin, and Pitirim Sorokin.

ADAM SMITH AND SIGMUND FREUD ON ECONOMIC FREEDOM AND SEXUAL FREEDOM

Adam Smith, the father of modern economics, offered insights on this subject. In his writings, he made a clear distinction between two societal classes: the leisure class and the working class. The leisure class ("people of fashion"), according to Smith, tends to favor a relaxed moral system. This is primarily because they possess the means to deal with the repercussions of their indulgent and extravagant lifestyles.

On the other hand, the working class or the common people generally adhere to a stricter moral code. This is because any deviation into excesses could lead to ruin due to their limited resources. Further, this is why Smith explained that religious sects flourish among the common people. These groups advocate a moral framework that is crucial for their well-being.

Smith further theorized about the potential impact of these moral systems on society. If a relaxed moral system is adopted universally, it could lead to societal collapse. This is due to the inability of the majority to handle the consequences of a sexually libertine lifestyle. However, if only the leisure class follows this system while the rest of society adheres to a stricter moral code, societal stability can be maintained, and society can prosper.

> In every civilised society, in every society where the distinction of ranks has once been completely established, there have been always two different schemes or systems of morality current at the same time; of which the one may be called the strict or austere; the other . . . , the loose system. The former is generally admired and revered by the common people: the latter commonly more esteemed and by what are called people of fashion . . . In the . . . loose system, luxury, wanton and even disorderly mirth, the pursuit of pleasure to some degree of intemperance, the breach of chastity, at least in one of the two sexes, etc., . . . , are generally treated with a good deal of indulgence, and are easily either excused or pardoned altogether.
>
> In the austere system, on the contrary, those excesses are regarded with the utmost abhorrence and detestation. The vices of levity are always ruinous to the common people, and a single week's thoughtlessness and dissipation is often sufficient to undo a poor workman for ever, and to drive him through despair upon committing the most enormous crimes. The wiser and better sort of the common people, therefore, have always the utmost abhorrence and detestation of such excesses, which their experience tells them are so immediately fatal to people of their condition.
>
> The disorder and extravagance of several years, on the contrary, will not always ruin a man of fashion, and people of that rank are very apt to consider the power of indulging in some degree of excess as one of the

advantages of their fortune, and the liberty of doing so without censure or reproach as one of the privileges which belong to their station. In people of their own station, therefore, they regard such excesses with but a small degree of disapprobation, and censure them either very slightly or not at all.[4]

Hence, according to Smith, a society can avoid collapse if most of its people have a strict moral code regardless of the smaller leisure class.

Sigmund Freud, the founder of psychoanalysis, proposed a theory that civilization (that is, an economically prosperous society) is a byproduct of repressed sexuality. He suggested that under the influence of 'civilized' morality, which restricts sexual freedom, the health and efficiency of individuals may be compromised. He further argued that the sacrifices demanded by such a morality could potentially harm individuals to such an extent that the very goals and ends of civilization could be indirectly threatened.

Freud viewed civilization as unstable and possibly self-defeating. He expressed his concerns in a letter to Albert Einstein, stating that he feared that by limiting sexual freedom, civilization might be heading towards the extinction of humanity. He considered total sexual abstinence, except within the confines of marriage, as a dangerous practice.[5]

Freud predicted that if sexual freedom were further restricted and the standards set by civilization were raised, it could lead to undesirable outcomes. He pointed out that when civilization demands abstinence until marriage from both sexes and lifelong abstinence for those who do not enter legal matrimony, it raises the question of "whether our 'civilized' sexual morality is worth the sacrifices it imposes upon us."[6]

---

4. Smith, *Wealth of Nations*, 1057–59.

5. https://www.public.asu.edu/~jmlynch/273/documents/FreudEinstein.pdf (accessed August 1, 2024).

6. Freud, *'Civilized' Sexual Morality and Modern Nervous Illness*, 204.

It's important to note that Freud was not a social scientist, and his theories were not empirically proven. However, he hoped that future research would provide evidence to support his theories.

THE UNWIN THESIS ON THE RELATIONSHIP BETWEEN SEXUAL FREEDOM AND ECONOMIC PROSPERITY

Joseph D. Unwin, a social anthropologist at Oxford and Cambridge University, set out to prove Freud's Theory. He collected data on eighty people groups[7] and about a dozen civilizations in history covering thousands of years.[8]

To examine Freud's theory that civilization is a consequence of suppressed sexuality, the scholar J. D. Unwin conducted extensive studies across numerous societies. His surprising findings caused a stir among scholars, including Unwin himself. Remarkably, all societies he studied showed a clear correlation between monogamy and the "expansive energy" of civilization.

Unwin, who did not hold any Christian convictions, abstained from making any moral assessments. He stated, "I offer no opinion about rightness or wrongness."[9] The fact that all the societies studied demonstrated a direct link between monogamy and the "expansive energy" of civilization was a revelation that left many, including Unwin himself, astounded. He said, "If you asked me why this is so, I reply that I do not know." He said, "No scientist does." You can describe the process and observe it, but you cannot explain it and with that one "has to be content."[10]

7. Unwin, *Hopousia or the Sexual and Economic Foundations of a New Society*, 98.

8. The civilizations he covered in depth included the Sumerians, Babylonian's, Athenians, Romans, Anglo-Saxons, and Protestant English. He also looked at Egyptians, Assyrians, Persians, Hindus, Chinese, Japanese, Sassanids, Arabs (Moors), and Teutons.

9. Unwin, *Hopousia or the Sexual and Economic Foundations of a New Society*, 85.

10. Unwin, *Hopousia or the Sexual and Economic Foundations of a New Society*, 103–04.

SEXUAL FREEDOM AND ECONOMIC FREEDOM

> In human records there is no instance of a society retaining its energy after a complete new generation has inherited a tradition which does not insist on pre-nuptial and post-nuptial continence . . . The evidence is that in the past a class has risen to a position of political dominance because of its great energy and that at the period of its rising, its sexual regulations have always been strict. It has retained its energy and dominated the society so long as its sexual regulations have demanded both pre-nuptial and post-nuptial continence . . . I know of no exceptions to these rules.[11]

Unwin appeared perplexed when attempting to explain the pattern, but it left such a profound impression on him that he suggested the establishment of an elite group of "alpha" citizens in a state known as Hopousia (Britain). These individuals, marked by their exceptional potential, would commit to chastity before marriage and adhere to strict monogamy post-marriage all in the interest of the Empire, which required their skills.[12] They were juxtaposed with the beta citizens who enjoyed sexual freedom. In Hopousia, there would be a shift towards decentralization, and individuals would be rewarded based on the fruits of their efforts, leading to the prosperity of the British nation.[13]

Interestingly, when England started colonizing India in 1757, a hundred years later, Indian thinkers were asking how a small island nation might have been so powerful. Many writers, including Ishwar Chandra Vidyasagar, concluded that it was the effective harnessing of sexual energy. A similar conclusion was reached by Unwin. While the elite classes in India at that time practiced polygamy, they realized that strict chastity and monogamy were important for society to develop and thrive and were the secret to

---

11. Unwin, *Hopousia or the Sexual and Economic Foundations of a New Society*, 84–85, 88–89.

12. Yancey, *The Lost Sex Study: If We Make a God of Sexuality, That God Will Fail in Ways That Affect the Whole Person and Perhaps the Whole Society.*, para 5.

13. Unwin, *Hopousia or the Sexual and Economic Foundations of a New Society*, 308, 10ff.

Britain's success. This resulted in India outlawing polygamy many decades later in 1955.[14]

What type of sexual regulations will society have? Unwin had seven categories of sexual regulations. Three of these regulations are pre-nuptial and four are for post-nuptial conduct. A society cannot just regulate post-nuptial conduct without also regulating pre-nuptial chastity. The prenuptial regulations include: "(1) men and women may be sexually free, (2) they may be subject to regulations which compel only an irregular or occasional continence, (3) under pain of punishment and even death the women may have to remain virgins until they are married."[15]

The four regulations after marriage include:

> Modified monogamy—the practice or circumstance of having one spouse at one time, the association being terminable by either party in accordance with the prevailing law or custom;
>
> Modified polygamy—the practice or circumstance of having more than one wife at one time, the wives being free to leave their husbands on terms laid down by law and custom;
>
> Absolute monogamy—the practice or circumstance of having one spouse at one time, but presupposing conditions whereby legally the wife is under the dominion of her husband and must confine her sexual qualities to him, under pain of punishment, for the whole of his or her life;
>
> Absolute polygamy—the practice or circumstance of having more than one wife at one time, these wives being compelled to confine their sexual qualities to their husband for the whole of their lives.[16]

In his study, he found that the 80 uncivilized societies fell into the 3 levels of prenuptial conduct as stated above. From this group, among the 10 societies that required prenuptial chastity,

14. Mangalwadi, *Sex: The Secret of the West's Economic Success*, lines 1–14.
15. Unwin, *Sex and Culture*, 341.
16. Unwin, *Sex and Culture*, 342.

they had either modified monogamy or modified polygamy, but none had absolute monogamy or absolute polygamy. He finds only one polygamous society that had productive social energy and that was the Moors.[17] This was because, the women the Moors married (Christians and Jews) came from a strong monogamous tradition, but the benefits lasted only one generation as the "mothers of a new generation had spent their early years in an absolutely polygamous environment."[18]

Unwin's causal story suggests that when desires, particularly sexual desires, are not fulfilled, it results in mental tension. This tension, according to Unwin, is then channeled into socially beneficial pursuits. This idea aligns with Freud's concept that civilization is built on the "sacrifices in gratification of the primitive impulses."[19]

Unwin posits that limiting sexual opportunities plays a crucial role in cultural advancement.[20] However, he also notes that the full impact of such limitations on culture may not be evident until at least a hundred years, or roughly three generations, have passed.[21] In his study, Unwin found only three instances of societies restricting sexual opportunities for three consecutive generations: the Athenians, Romans, and English. According to Unwin, these restrictions led to significant societal growth and advancement.[22]

When sexual opportunity is limited, "ardent men explore new lands . . . thoughtful men begin to look beyond the horizon that their fathers regarded as the limits of the world. Commerce is extended; foreign settlements are established; colonies founded."[23]

"[E]ven if other factors also are indispensable and operating, no social energy can be displayed unless the sexual opportunity is

---

17. Unwin, *Sex and Culture*, 343.
18. Unwin, *Sex and Culture*, 368.
19. Freud, *A General Introduction to Psychoanalysis*, 27.
20. Unwin, *Sex and Culture*, 317.
21. Unwin, *Sex and Culture*, 326.
22. Unwin, *Sex and Culture*, 430.
23. Unwin, *Sexual Regulations and Cultural Behaviour*, 20.

limited."[24] Unwin went so far as to state "[I]f we know what sexual regulations a society has adopted, we can prophesy the pattern of its cultural behaviour."[25]

Finally, Unwin saw that it was **impossible** to have both sexual freedom and high culture. "Any human society is free to choose either to display great energy or to enjoy sexual freedom; the evidence is that it cannot do both for more than one generation."[26] Total collapse takes about three generations.[27]

UNWIN AND THE ROLE OF FEMALE EMANCIPATING MOVEMENTS IN SEXUAL LIBERATION

So, what causes increasing sexual energy in societies that initially restricted sexual opportunity? According to Unwin, to limit sexual opportunity, societies restrict women and children. That women are subjected to domination by their husbands. "In the past, too, the greatest energy has been displayed only by those societies which have reduced their sexual opportunity to a minimum by the adoption of absolute monogamy. In every case the women and children were reduced to the level of legal nonentities, sometimes also to the level of chattels, always to the level of mere appendages of the male estate."[28]

Hence to correct this injustice, reforms are introduced to liberate women, but in the process, it also expands sexual opportunity. "A female emancipating movement is a cultural phenomenon of unfailing regularity; it appears to be the necessary outcome of absolute monogamy. The subsequent loss of social energy after the emancipation of women, which is sometimes emphasized, has been due not to the emancipation but to the extension of sexual

24. Unwin, *Sex and Culture*, 320.
25. Unwin, *Sexual Regulations and Cultural Behaviour*, 6.
26. Unwin, *Sex and Culture*, 412.
27. Unwin, *Sex and Culture*, 370.
28. Unwin, *Sex and Culture*, 431.

opportunity that has **always** accompanied it. In human records **there is no instance** of female emancipation which has not been accompanied by an extension of sexual opportunity" (emphasis added).[29] Unwin further suggests that there may be a way to restrict sexual opportunity under other conditions without subjugating women but has not seen it in his examples.[30] For these reasons, Unwin suggests that restraining sexual opportunities for females is more important than for males.[31]

For example, let's look at Rome starting over a century before Christ:

> By the late Hellenistic Age, this had resulted in a metamorphosis in the position of women. Equality for women extended beyond politics into economic life, and in some occupations such as plumbing they came to dominate. The rate of divorce increased enormously, and the power 'of the paterfamilias was shaken to its foundations and eventually swept away altogether.' 'The meek and henpecked Roman husband was already a stock comedy figure in the great days of the Second Punic War.' This changing relationship led Cato the Censor to protest bitterly, 'All other men rule over women; but we Romans, who rule all men, are ruled by our women.' Equality had progressed to the point that by the late Empire a woman who married retained her property, 'and, legally, the man had not even the right to enjoy the income from it.'[32]

Similarly in the U.S., the female emancipation movement came not from a desire to free oneself from the Christian past, but from the Enlightenment past. Starting in the Age of Reason (enlightenment), family law began to evolve. "The Age of Reason saw man as reason incarnate, and woman as emotion and will, and therefore inferior."[33] Further, during the Enlightenment, marriage

---

29. Unwin, *Sex and Culture*, 344–45.
30. Unwin, *Sex and Culture*, 381.
31. Unwin, *Sex and Culture*, 323.
32. Marina, *Egalitarianism and Empire*, 10.
33. Rushdoony, *The Institutes of Biblical Law*, 349.

was not seen as sacramental or covenantal, but rather as a voluntary bargain between two parties themselves,[34] holding that God was not an active agent in these affairs. The changing ideas impacted the early 19th-century law books and were instrumental in decreasing the bargaining power of the wife in the marriage relationship. For example:

> The legal theory is, that marriage makes the husband and wife one person, and that person is the husband. He is the substantive and she the adjective. In a word, there is scarcely a legal act of any description, which she is competent to perform. The common reason assigned for this legal disfranchisement of the wife, is, that there may be an indissoluble union of interest between the parties. In other words, lest the wife might be sometimes tempted to assert rights in opposition to her husband, the law humanely divests her of rights.[35]

In one case, when the wife was charged with the murder of her illegitimate child by failing to provide proper food, the judge in the case talks about the wife as the servant of her husband.[36] These changes can be seen in the early 19th century law books and the changes were instrumental in decreasing the bargaining power of the wife in the marriage. Instead of biblical submission, it became subjugation. In the U.S., this led to corrective actions during the late 1800s and early 1900s with the women's emancipation movement, eventually culminating in the sexual revolution of the mid-1900s. The sexual revolution period saw the introduction of easy divorce laws, acceptance of sex outside of marriage, abortion liberalization, and more.[37] If Unwin's theory holds, it could result in economic collapse within three generations.

34. Witte, *From Sacrament to Contract: Marriage, Religion, and Law in the Western Tradition, Family, Religion, and Culture*, 197.

35. Walker, *Introduction to American Law: Designed as a First Book for Students*, 223. This language carries through until the 10th edition of this book, which was published in 1895.

36. Wharton, *An Exposition of the Laws Relating to the Women of England: Showing Their Rights, Remedies, and Responsibilities in Every Position of Life*, 163.

37. Bose, *A Contractual Look at the Role of Religion in the Stability of*

A similar observation can also be seen in the Arab Empire showing how the emancipation of women eventually led to its decline.

> An increase in the influence of women in public life has often been associated with national decline. The later Romans complained that, although Rome ruled the world, women ruled Rome. In the tenth century, a similar tendency was observable in the Arab Empire, the women demanding admission to the professions hitherto monopolised by men. 'What,' wrote the contemporary historian, Ibn Bessam, 'have the professions of clerk, tax-collector or preacher to do with women? These occupations have always been limited to men alone.' Many women practised law, while others obtained posts as university professors. There was an agitation for the appointment of female judges, which, however, does not appear to have succeeded.
>
> Soon after this period [which also saw a relaxation of sexual morals], government and public order collapsed, and foreign invaders overran the country. The resulting increase in confusion and violence made it unsafe for women to move unescorted in the streets, with the result that this feminist movement collapsed.[38]

When studying the Cretans, Unwin notes, that when women achieve high positions, their rise has "been accompanied by the adoption of a less rigorous form of marriage."[39]

UNWIN AND THE ROLE OF CHRISTIANITY

What role did Christianity play in societies that were converted by missionaries? According to Unwin, he found that societies became less strict regarding sexual morality not just in the modern era but also in earlier eras.

Marriage, 57.
    38. Chubb, *The Fate of Empires and Search for Survival*, 15.
    39. Unwin, *Monogamy as a Condition of Social Energy*, 665.

> In modern times a form of Catholic [Universal, not Roman Catholic] Christianity is being widely disseminated throughout the uncivilized world; and, though Christians may dislike it, the effect of their teaching upon uncivilized societies, is not to tighten but to loosen the sexual regulations. The reason is that the Christians merely forgive and forbid those sexual lapses which under native rule were effectually prevented.[40]

In Christian terms, what Christians consider as "biblical marriage" Unwin calls "Pauline absolute monogamy," and he identifies it with the Protestant Reformation. He states that Paul absorbed ideas from Roman elements and Gamaliel: "In each case the ideas were those of absolute monogamy; and in this manner some implications of absolute monogamy have been petrified in a Christian ideal."[41]

Unwin attributes the modern success of Western Civilization to "Pauline absolute monogamy," but notes that every society that practices absolute monogamy ultimately relaxes its rules and collapses soon afterward. Unwin finds the history of marriage customs the same. "Each society reduced its sexual opportunity to a minimum and, displaying great social energy, flourished greatly. Then it extended its sexual opportunity; its energy decreased, and faded away. **The one outstanding feature of the whole story is its unrelieved monotony**" (emphasis added).[42]

Reformed Western churches have long adhered to the concept of "Pauline absolute monogamy" for 500 years. However, they are currently shifting towards the broader principles of the Universal Church from the past. That Church prioritizes expanding its congregation, showing limited concern for the sexual conduct of its members, except when dispensing forgiveness or verbal prohibitions. This shift, though regrettable, reflects a return to traditional Christian norms.

---

40. Unwin, *Sex and Culture*, 376.
41. Unwin, *Sex and Culture*, 375.
42. Unwin, *Sex and Culture*, 381.

Figure 1-1 illustrates the Unwin thesis. It is an attempt to illustrate the economic and sexual freedom possibilities in a simple two-by-two matrix. The Unwin thesis is different than the freedom hypothesis which suggests that economic freedom and sexual freedom should be complementary and that freedom, whether economic or sexual, is desirable. The individual should not be restrained by the state in any economic activities or sexual activities that are based on mutual consent.

The upper-left quadrant represents situations with high levels of sexual freedom, but low levels of economic freedom. The lower-right quadrant represents low levels of sexual freedom matched with high levels of economic freedom. The upper-right and lower-left quadrants reflect matching levels of sexual and economic freedom accordingly. The freedom hypothesis is consistent with the upper- right quadrant with high sexual freedom and high economic freedom, however, according to Unwin, this is a temporary equilibrium. The lower-right quadrant is consistent with the Unwin Thesis of high economic freedom and low sexual freedom. Combinations of sexual freedom and less economic freedom in the upper-left are typically found in primitive societies.[43,44] The combination in the lower-left is also a possible quadrant and likely typical of autocratic societies with the preference of the ruler or elites dominating society, but that would be unstable.

	Not Economically Free	**Economically Free**
Sexually Free	Primitive Societies	Freedom Hypothesis, Unstable per Unwin Thesis
Not Sexually Free	Totalitarianism (unstable)	**Unwin Thesis**

Figure 1-1: Economic and Sexual Freedom Possibilities Matrix.

43. Malinowski, *The Sexual Life of Savages in North-Western Melanesia; an Ethnographic Account of Courtship, Marriage, and Family Life among the Natives of the Trobriand Islands, British New Guinea*, 1–480.

44. Rachewiltz, *Black Eros : Sexual Customs of Africa from Prehistory to the Present Day*, 13–283.

PITIRIM SOROKIN ON THE IMPACT OF SEXUAL FREEDOM

Pitirim Sorokin, the founder of Harvard's Sociology Department, builds on Unwin's work. Sorokin's survey of literature over time found that during medieval times, literature focused on sacred topics and any discussion of sexual immorality was condemnatory. At the start of the 14th century, secular literature started dominating writings. Any violation of God's laws in these writings were seen as tragic, with only a few pieces of literature being strictly erotic. Since the 19th century, writings have focused on what Pitirim calls the "social sewers" dealing with criminals, prostitutes, disloyal parents, delinquents, and so on. The portrayal of sexual love and marriage also goes through a transformation with abnormal forms being extolled, the "perverse, vulgar, picaresque, exotic, and even monstrous forms,—the sex adventures of urbanized cavemen and rapists, the loves of adulterers and fornicators, of masochists and sadists, of prostitutes, mistresses, play boys, and entertainment personalities."[45] Sorokin finds that the late 20th century U.S. literature degraded later relative to Europe.

Table 1-1: Erotic representations over time based on 200,000 pictures and sculptures in Europe.[46]

10th to 13th century	Nil
14th and 15th century	0.4 percent
16th century	10.8 percent
17th century	21.3 percent
18th century	36.4 percent
19th century	25.1 percent
20th century (till 1920)	38.1 percent

Similarly, Sorokin finds paintings and sculptures had less sensually nude bodies but over time nudity increases (see Table

45. Sorokin, *Sane Sex Order*, 19.
46. Sorokin, *Sane Sex Order*, 22.

1–1). This mirrored the loosening of sexual morals in society and a decline in family stability. His main thesis here is that as society becomes more decadent, sensual nudity increases in the visual arts in all cultures. This same pattern is also seen in music and other arts.

Sorokin suggests two generalizations as to why there is a relationship between sexual life and creative growth or decline of society. "The regime," Sorokin writes, "that permits chronically excessive, illicit, and disorderly sex activities contributes to the decline of cultural creativity, [while] the regime that confines sexual life within socially sanctioned marriage . . . provides an environment more favorable for creative growth of the society than does the regime of free or disorderly sex relationships which neither morally disapproves nor legally prohibits premarital and extramarital liaisons."[47] Using Unwin's findings and his own, he writes that, "there is no example [in history] of a community which has retained its high position on the cultural scale after less rigorous sexual customs have replaced more restricting ones."[48] The loosening of sexual regulations in various late-stage civilizations were all associated with a decline in creative vigor. He provides evidence from Soviet Russia.

In Soviet Russia, Vladimir Lenin and the Bolsheviks were advocating a theory about sex, known as the "Glass of Water" theory. They asserted that sexual desire is as ordinary and essential as the need for food or water. This perspective led to significant changes in the Soviet legal system to reflect this viewpoint. However, this theory quickly fell out of favor as society collapsed, and the societal norms in the Soviet Union shifted quickly towards a more conservative stance on sexual morality, at least superficially (More details in Chapter 2).

Sorokin further argues that while it might seem that relaxed sexual standards would sustainably facilitate population growth, the reality is quite different. He finds that such societies may experience a population decline within a generation or two. The reason, he suggests, is that the responsibility of raising children could

---

47. Sorokin, *Sane Sex Order*, 84.
48. Sorokin, *Sane Sex Order*, 88.

hinder individuals from achieving their personal goals as children are increasingly seen as a burden.

To substantiate his argument, Sorokin points to historical evidence from various aristocratic families in Europe. These families, known for their libertine sexual practices, saw many of their family lines become extinct. For instance, in England, between the years 1611 and 1819, a total of 1527 baronetcies were established. By the dawn of the 20th century, only 43% of these had survived.[49]

Sorokin's analysis implies that the trends observed within individual families can have broader societal implications. The patterns of population growth and decline within families, influenced by their sexual norms, can reflect and impact the demographic trends of societies at large impacting growth and prosperity.

Sorokin writes, "[w]hatever may be the virtues of age, they cannot compensate for the vitality, vigor, courage, daring, elasticity, and creativity of the young. A nation largely composed of middle-aged or elderly people enfeebles itself physically, mentally, and socially, and moves toward the end of its creative mission and leadership."[50] Following Sorokin's work, the literature exploring the relationship between sexual and economic freedom basically disappeared till more recently.

CONCLUSION

In conclusion, early scholars in this field, particularly Unwin, observed that societies that expanded sexual freedom tended to face economic decline over time. Further, if they restricted sexual freedom, societies experienced economic vitality and growth. Economic vitality and growth are the hallmarks of society that allow for economic freedom. Hence, while early writers believed that economic and sexual freedom were substitutes, they were unable to articulate a clear reason why they were substitutes. As I proceed in this book, I will lay the ground work to explain the

---

49. Sorokin, *Sane Sex Order*, 70.
50. Sorokin, *Sane Sex Order*, 71–72.

causal relationship between economic and sexual freedom. But first, in the next chapter, I will examine two historical episodes that illustrate the detrimental impact of sexual freedom on prosperity.

2

Micro and Macro Episode in the History of Sexual Freedom and its Impact

Like a city whose walls are broken through is a person who lacks self-control.

PROVERBS 25:28 (NIV)

IN THIS CHAPTER, I will look at two episodes in history to see the impact of sexual freedom on people's energy and productivity. As Unwin noted, increasing sexual freedom curtails expansive energy, eventually resulting in the loss of civilization. Two episodes will be discussed, including a micro case (HMS Bounty) and a macro case (Soviet Union). While these episodes are not over long periods, the HMS Bounty and the Soviet Union showcase how changes in sexual freedom can impact societal energy quickly.

EPISODE 1: HMS BOUNTY

Captain William Bligh oversaw a ship called the HMS Bounty that set sail for Tahiti on December 23, 1787. His mission was to collect breadfruit plants from Tahiti and take them to the West Indies.

The goal was to grow the plants and use them as a source of food for the slaves working on the plantations. The breadfruit was easy to grow and provided food all year round. However, Bligh faced an unexpected challenge. The plants needed more time to grow before they could survive the journey to the West Indies. In response, Bligh made an unusual decision for a Royal Navy commander: he allowed his crew to live on land and interact regularly with the local population. Further, numerous women were allowed on board to stay with the men, and, at times multiple women with a man. However, this decision turned out to be a mistake. The crew went from enforced celibacy and harsh discipline during their travel to Tahiti, to a period of self-indulgence and laziness.

The ship had to remain docked on the island of Tahiti for five months before it could set sail on April 5th, 1789. Unfortunately, this prolonged period of idleness proved to be disastrous for the expedition, contrary to the expectations of Captain Bligh. The local culture on the island was non-Christian and was not supportive of hard work. Instead, it was devoted to indulgence in immoral activities, which made the situation worse. Bligh was horrified by some of the sexual practices of the Polynesians. This included sodomy, wife sharing, publicly "deflowering" young girls as young as seven, and so on. The sexual promiscuity of the crew of the Bounty resulted in the spread of venereal disease. Further, the men of the Bounty did not maintain the ship during this time of indulgence resulting in the unused spare sails being found rotten and mildewed, parts of the ship decaying, smaller boats being in poor shape, the bower anchor being rotted through, and so on.[1]

For more than five months, with all the seductive delights of one of the most beautiful islands in the world freely and daily available, he left them if not to their own devices then under the ever-slackening supervision of his officers in whom he had no confidence-while he spent most of his time enjoying life with the royal family, studying the people, the flora and fauna, and watching his garden grow.[2]

---

1. Hough, *Captain Bligh and Mr Christian: The Men and the Mutiny*, 123, 26.
2. Hough, *Captain Bligh and Mr Christian: The Men and the Mutiny*, 127.

Bligh was not particularly interested in religion. This is evident from his letters to his wife and report on the mutiny, which does not contain any references to God, Christ, or Divine Providence. He rather believed in "science," which was a common belief among many "enlightened gentlemen" during his time. This led Bligh to overlook the spiritual and cultural risks of allowing his crew to reside among a native culture known for its idleness and sexual promiscuity.[3] Even in port, sailors typically remained on board. Bligh carried huge risks by allowing his crew to mix with the natives.[4]

Influenced by the locals' promiscuous culture, both seamen and officers aboard the ship formed relationships with local women. The local chiefs encouraged these connections, viewing the British as useful allies in their inter-tribal conflicts. Many crew members underwent tattooing rituals and were integrated into local clans. Fletcher Christian, a sailing master appointed by Bligh, even married a local woman. Ironically, Christian later led the mutiny against Bligh. The crew members seemed to have had "no Christian restraint, self-control, or any other kind of spiritual convictions." The temptation of sin is difficult for even committed Christians to overcome, but for "practical atheists like the crew of the Bounty it had devastating effects."[5]

Bligh did not foresee the impact of these hedonistic months on his crew. Three weeks after the Bounty departed Tahiti, half of the crew, led by Fletcher Christian, mutinied. They abandoned Captain Bligh and the loyal crew members in a small boat and returned to Tahiti. Bligh then undertook a heroic sea voyage of 3,600 nautical miles to Timor.[6] The Bounty went back to Tahiti, where some crew members stayed. However, Christian, along with eight other crewmen, six Tahitian men (two from Tubai), and eleven Tahitian women, left Tahiti, fearing a chase by the Royal Navy.[7]

---

3. Marinov, *A Tale of Two Islands*, 4.
4. Lummis, *Pitcairn Island: Life and Death in Eden*, 13.
5. Marinov, *A Tale of Two Islands*, 4.
6. Marinov, *A Tale of Two Islands*, 4.
7. Hough, *Captain Bligh and Mr Christian: The Men and the Mutiny*, 204, 05.

In January 1790, they found Pitcairn Island and decided to settle there, eventually burning the Bounty. Each crewman was paired with a woman, while three women were shared with the native men. Soon after, two women died—one from the crew and one from the natives—sparking new conflicts as there was an attempt to reassign one of the women from the natives to the crewmen.

What followed demonstrated how individuals, devoid of Christian principles, can create a living hell. Despite having ample food, water, tools, seeds from the Bounty, and plenty of land, the group stranded on Pitcairn Island descended into chaos. The optimal climate did little to prevent the ensuing strife.[8] Fights broke out among the men, and the Tahitians rebelled against the British crewmen. In the resulting conflict, all six Tahitian men and five crewmen, including Christian, were killed.[9]

Out of the remaining four crewmen, two had started brewing alcohol from native plants. This alcohol was very potent. Heavy drinking became the norm among the surviving men, which made life miserable for the women. The women also lost respect for the white men whose behavior was uncivilized. The women tried to revolt and kill the men several times but were unsuccessful; they were forgiven by the men who did not want to lose their companionship.[10] Some of them even attempted to escape the island on a crude raft, but it was unable to leave the bay where it was built. The women also plotted to murder the white men before leaving on the raft.

One of the men almost died of drunkenness and ended up committing suicide. Another heavy drinker was killed by the other two men for threatening to kill everyone on the island and steal their wives. The two remaining men started reforming themselves and rediscovered their Christian faith. They gave up alcohol and forbade the women from drinking alcohol.[11] Then they gave themselves wholly to the Christian faith and spread it in the

8. Marinov, *A Tale of Two Islands*, 4.
9. Lummis, *Pitcairn Island: Life and Death in Eden*, 57–82.
10. Lummis, *Pitcairn Island: Life and Death in Eden*, 87.
11. Hough, *Captain Bligh and Mr Christian: The Men and the Mutiny*, 267.

small community. One man, Edward Young, was soon to die of asthma. For this reason, John Adams, aka Alexander Smith, who was scarcely literate, took daily reading lessons so he could lead the women and children in the Christian faith. Out of the original 15 men who created the colony, only one remained.

John Adams, the only man stranded on an island with nine women and children, through the miraculously preserved ship's Bible and prayer book, organized regular weekly services to teach Christianity to the colony. Finally, after years of misery, hatred, sexual promiscuity, and death, there was peace and rebuilding on the island. Emphasis was placed on reading and writing with the source of morals coming from the Bible. Daily prayers and Sunday services were practiced.[12] When Quaker Mayhew Folger rediscovered Pitcairn, he found the small colony recovering from years of suffering, building a new culture and civilization based on their Christian faith. Adams shared with him the collapse of morals and the death, murder, or suicide of many of the members before their conversion and reformation based on the Bible that brought about peace and stability. A few years later, two British warships arrived in Pitcairn, and the commanders of the boats assured the dwellers that John Adams, the patriarch, would not be arrested. After seeing their island, they further thought that it would be 'an act of great cruelty and inhumanity' to arrest him and take him back to Britain for court martial and execution.[13]

Sexual libertinism led to a dysfunctional society, despite geographical advantages that should have fostered economic prosperity. The economic and societal collapse was only reversed through a revival rooted in adherence to Biblical teachings.

---

12. Lummis, *Pitcairn Island: Life and Death in Eden*, 91, 123.
13. Hough, *Captain Bligh and Mr Christian: The Men and the Mutiny*, 274f.

EPISODE 2: BOLSHEVIK'S SEXUAL REVOLUTION IN THE SOVIET UNION

In 1918, after the Bolsheviks seized control of Russia and executed the Christian Czar Nicholas II, his wife Alexandra, and their five children, they initiated a legal sexual revolution to dismantle the moral framework of Tsarist rule. Marxism believes that women were oppressed due to unpaid labor and strict sexual conduct for women. Whereas men, especially upper-class men, could get away with adultery, women were held to a stricter standard. This double standard was seen as antiquated and tied to the role of the family as an economic unit. That is, a woman's chastity is important to transfer wealth across generations through natural heirs. This restriction was seen as the root cause of the oppression of women. For this reason, the family had to be replaced. The sexual revolution was to be removed from monetary considerations. Collective kitchens, childcare facilities, and laundries were to be established to allow for payment for labor.

The Marxists believed making divorce difficult protected property rights and trapped individuals in unhappy marriages while simultaneously exploiting individuals. Marriage was a prison that needed to be opened. Within 6 weeks after the Bolsheviks obtained power, they passed a decree to allow for easy divorce and removed the church's involvement in marriage. The 1918 family code saw marriage as a secular state contract instead of a religious affair. Divorce laws were liberalized, and marriages were performed without respect to sex. This resulted in a huge increase in divorce. Further, in 1918, adoption was abolished to stop the creation of new families as they were seen as reflecting the old way of life.[14] The Bolsheviks removed any distinction between legitimate and illegitimate children. All alleged fathers had to pay alimony. Anti-sodomy laws were repealed. Transgenderism was also accepted.[15] There was a resulting shift away from strict

---

14. Wardle, *The "Withering Away" of Marriage: Some Lessons from the Bolshevik Family Law Reforms in Russia, 1917–1926*, 483.

15. Egan, *The Bolsheviks and the Sexual Revolution*, 39.

monogamy or marriage among the young with only a minority still seeing marriage as the ideal family structure.

A few years later, in 1920, the Soviets legalized abortion with no restriction and was seen by the revolutionaries as important for women's rights. Further in 1920, cohabitation was legitimized and existed as the *de facto* marriage. Marriage was reduced to "the status of nonmarital unions" and "nonmarital unions to the legal status of marriage."[16] While divorce by mutual consent was easy, divorce by one party required court involvement. The 1926 code also permitted unilateral divorce through a postcard. Marriage and divorce were just seen as a private agreement and not a lifelong union, no different than cohabitation in many ways.[17]

Till 1935, all adult sexual behavior was decriminalized; this included adultery, homosexual behavior, polygamy (except in Muslim areas), and abolishment of illegitimacy regarding children born out of wedlock.

During the first stage of the Revolution, its leaders deliberately attempted to destroy marriage and the family. Free love was glorified by the official 'glass of water' theory: if a person is thirsty, so went the Party line, it is immaterial what glass he uses when satisfying his thirst; it is equally unimportant how he satisfies his sex hunger. The legal distinction between marriage and casual sexual intercourse was abolished. The Communist law spoke only of 'contracts' between males and females for the satisfaction of their desires either for an indefinite or a definite period—a year, a month, a week, or even for a single night. One could marry and divorce as many times as desired . . . Bigamy and even polygamy were permissible under the new provisions. Abortion was facilitated in state institutions. Premarital relations were praised, and extramarital relations were considered normal.[18]

---

16. Wardle, *The "Withering Away" of Marriage: Some Lessons from the Bolshevik Family Law Reforms in Russia, 1917-1926*, 484.

17. Wardle, *The "Withering Away" of Marriage: Some Lessons from the Bolshevik Family Law Reforms in Russia, 1917-1926*, 482.

18. Sorokin, *Sane Sex Order*, 91.

In 1923, Grigorii Batkis, who was the director of the Institute for Social Hygiene Moscow stated the Bolshevik position: 'It declares the absolute non-interference of the state and society into sexual matters, so long as nobody is injured, and no one's interests are encroached upon.' A modern left-leaning libertarian position.[19]

During this time, a literary correspondent observed a societal phenomenon where men exhibited a propensity for frequently changing their wives, a behavior that mirrored their enthusiastic consumption of the recently reintroduced vodka. In rural villages, it was common for men to switch wives swiftly, with some men having as many as twenty wives; they spent a week or a month with each in turn. Young peasant men viewed marriage as an exhilarating game, changing wives as the seasons changed. It was not uncommon for a twenty-year-old boy to have been married to three or four different women. Some men even took on "summer brides."[20]

However, this trend of frequent marital changes led to an increase in abandonment, forced divorces, blackmail, and extortion. Men who found new opportunities or positions often casually discarded their long-time wives. This period marked a significant shift in marital practices, with Christian notions of marriage and commitment giving way to a more transient and changeable approach. The societal implications of these changes were profound, affecting not just the individuals involved but also the broader community.

Further, since the state was seen as being responsible for raising children, parents abandoned their children as they did not want to be bothered by raising them. Wives who were abandoned by men faced great pressure to provide for their children which naturally resulted in the abandonment or abuse of their young. Women also were not in a good financial situation given the potential of multiple fathers, who themselves were not able to pay alimony. Many women turned to prostitution to pay the bills. Soviet society saw a rise in female-led households. However, many children

---

19. Egan, *The Bolsheviks and the Sexual Revolution*, 39.

20. Wardle, *The "Withering Away" of Marriage: Some Lessons from the Bolshevik Family Law Reforms in Russia, 1917–1926*, 492.

were also abandoned. These abandoned children numbered in the millions resulting in horrific conditions. These included forming gangs, begging, stealing, murdering, prostitution, and so on. These gangs attacked individuals and firms.[21]

Further, there was a declining birthrate and an unbalanced sex ratio with male numbers falling very low due to purges, internal wars, famines, and so on. To reverse the looming disaster a profamily posture was instituted.[22]

With the decay of society, Stalin saw in 1936 that the Bolshevik sexual revolution was a mistake and sought to return to the old values primarily due to the looming war with National Socialist Germany. In 1934, anti-sodomy laws had been reintroduced, and homosexuality was seen as a "bourgeois degeneracy." In 1936, the family code abolished the communal kitchens, laundries, and restaurants were closed. Divorce was discouraged by fines and was made difficult to obtain. Women with large families were awarded medals and payments. Pregnancy leave, childcare, and longer maternity leave were given.[23]

During 1935 and 1936, a vigorous campaign was conducted across the nation. This campaign targeted sexual promiscuity, hasty and casual marriages, bigamy, adultery, and the sexual exploitation of women. In 1944, additional restrictions were imposed on divorce to strengthen marriage and the family while cohabitation was delegalized. Emphasis was placed on responsibility, procreation, and child-rearing. The importance of stable marriages, large families, and self-discipline was elevated. This period marked a significant transformation in the regime's values, with a clear inclination towards original family structures and responsibilities. The reforms were mostly successful such that by the mid-20th century Soviet society displayed "a more monogamic, stable, and

---

21. Wardle, *The "Withering Away" of Marriage: Some Lessons from the Bolshevik Family Law Reforms in Russia, 1917–1926*, 493.

22. Piano, *Autocratic Family Policy*, 248–49.

23. Wardle, *The "Withering Away" of Marriage: Some Lessons from the Bolshevik Family Law Reforms in Russia, 1917–1926*, 486.

Victorian family and marriage life."[24] However, high abortion and divorce rates persisted.[25] This suggests that a complete reversal is difficult to implement by elites once societal norms have shifted for the worse and are bound to have continued negative economic consequences.

CONCLUSION

In the two episodes examined, societies of any size that diverge from Christian principles of marriage and child-rearing tend to face economic and societal decline. Conversely, when these societies revert to strict monogamy or adhere to Biblical standards of marriage, they experience improvements, leading to prosperity and stability. These two episodes tie in with Unwin's thesis about the link between sexual freedom and expansive civilizations. While Unwin suggested longer time frames for economic collapse and sustained economic growth (three generations), under certain circumstances the changes in sexual freedom can impact economic outcomes much sooner. In the next chapter, I will look at the sexual revolution in the U.S. and focus on the impact of Alfred Kinsey's research.

---

24. Sorokin, *Sane Sex Order*, 92.
25. Wardle, *The "Withering Away" of Marriage: Some Lessons from the Bolshevik Family Law Reforms in Russia, 1917–1926*, 496.

3

History of Sexual Revolution in the U.S.

The Impact of Alfred Kinsey

Drink water from your own cistern, And running water from your own well. Should your fountains be dispersed abroad, Streams of water in the streets? Let them be only your own, And not for strangers with you. Let your fountain be blessed, And rejoice with the wife of your youth. *As a loving deer and a graceful doe, Let her breasts satisfy you at all times; And always be enraptured with her love.*

Proverbs 5:15–19 (NKJV)

A HUNDRED YEARS AGO, the United States was sexually unfree. Today it is sexually free, with some states freer than others. The history of the sexual revolution in the United States is typically traced back to Alfred Kinsey in the mid-1900s. However, one can easily trace the sexual revolution back even further. In a weighty tome, E. Michael Jones traces the modern sexual revolution to the Enlightenment era starting with Marquis de Sade.[1] If one uses the Bible as

---

1. Jones, *Libido Dominandi: Sexual Liberation and Political Control*, 19–32.

a source, we can see the sexual revolution playing out in the book of Genesis, the first book of the Bible, in the stories of Sodom and Gomorrah, and even in the pre-flood period. Hence the idea that sexual liberation is a product of the modern era is simply not true. In this chapter, we will trace the sexual revolution in the U.S.

The study of human sexuality in the U.S. and more broadly can be categorized into two distinct periods: the era before Kinsey's research and the era that followed it. In this chapter, we will focus primarily on the latter era with reference made to the earlier era.

In the Pre-Kinsey Era, the common law, which was heavily influenced by biblical authority, was prevalent. During this time, the only form of legal sexual activity was marital coitus. The laws related to sex were primarily designed to control what was "sin." Those who violated these laws were subjected to penalties, imprisonment, and in some cases, even capital punishment.

The post-Kinsey Era marked a significant shift in the legal perspective on human sexuality. The introduction of the "Model Penal Code" by the American Law Institute (ALI) in 1962[2] was based on "scientific authority" rather than religious teachings. In this era, consent became the determining factor for the legality of sexual activities. Instead of punishing the offenders, they were to be paroled, pardoned, or treated as patients.[3]

Under the Common Law, various sexual behaviors were strictly regulated and often criminalized. These included sex before marriage (fornication), sex outside of marriage (adultery), public sex display (exhibitionism), sodomy (viewed as a deviant behavior), seduction (both breach of promise and alienation of affection), abortion (classified as murder), child sex (rape, statutory rape), and pornography (considered obscene).

However, this perspective underwent a significant transformation. The current scientific approach acknowledges that **all children are sexual beings**. It also posits that all sexual activity is either legal or managed therapeutically, with penalties being considerably lighter than in the common law era.

---

2. Numerous drafts and revisions were completed and sent out before this.
3. *Aids and IV Drug Use*, 186ff.

THE SEX RESEARCH OF KINSEY

In 1948, the findings of the Kinsey team located at Indiana University revealed some startling facts about the sexual behaviors of American men. According to their research, a staggering 95 percent of American men were found to be engaging in sexual activities that were considered illegal under the laws at the time. This included a wide range of behaviors such as premarital sex, with upwards of 98 percent of men admitting to sex before marriage with lower numbers if college-bound (67%).[4]

The study also found that 69 percent of white men had at least one encounter with a prostitute,[5] while 50 percent confessed to committing adultery. Surprisingly, up to 50 percent of farm boys admitted to having sexual relations with animals.[6]

In terms of sexual preferences, the study found that 10 to 37 percent of men had homosexual tendencies at some point in their lives.[7] Furthermore, 46 percent of men reported having "reacted to" both sexes at some stage.[8]

The societal norms and legal structures of the post-World War II era in America were primarily designed to protect the family unit, with the father considered the cornerstone. However, the groundbreaking research conducted by Alfred Kinsey painted a vastly different picture of the American father, challenging the prevailing beliefs of the time.

Kinsey's findings suggested that the image of the father as the moral compass and protector of the family was not entirely accurate. Instead, he found that fathers were engaging in a range of sexual behaviors that contradicted the societal expectations of their roles. This revelation was met with shock, but the data presented by Kinsey was largely accepted without question, hailed as a

---

4. Kinsey, et al., *Sexual Behavior in the Human Male*, 552.
5. Kinsey, et al., *Sexual Behavior in the Human Male*, 597.
6. Kinsey, et al., *Sexual Behavior in the Human Male*, 671.
7. Kinsey, et al., *Sexual Behavior in the Human Male*, 585, 87.
8. Kinsey, et al., *Sexual Behavior in the Human Male*, 656.

scientific breakthrough that would revolutionize our understanding of human sexuality.

Morris Ernst, the founder of the American Civil Liberties Union (ACLU), echoed this sentiment in 1948. He pointed out the irony in the fact that while our laws and customs were designed to protect the family with the father at its base, the reality of the father's sexual behavior was quite different from what the public had supposed. "The whole of our laws and customs are designed to protect the family, and at the base of the family is the father," but the father is "quite different from anything the general public had supposed."[9]

This new perspective on the sexual behavior of American fathers, which portrayed them as adventurous and promiscuous, played a significant role in the radical changes that swept through society in the 1960s. The introduction of the contraceptive pill in 1968 marked the beginning of an era characterized by widespread adultery, divorce, and venereal disease. This period also saw a rise in skepticism towards the traditional role of the father, leading to an increase in fathers abandoning their families. Consequently, the responsibility of raising children often fell to unrelated boyfriends or the state.

A few years later, the Kinsey team's research unveiled some striking findings about the sexual behaviors of women. In a detailed breakdown, Kinsey found that among white women, 50 percent had sex before marriage with a majority of them having no regrets,[10] and about 25 percent committed adultery and many more considered it.[11] Further studies from Kinsey's team found that among college-educated women, over 80 percent of single women had an induced abortion with the number smaller for high school-educated women (over 60 percent).[12] Among women who married early, 38 percent had induced abortions (2.4 per women

---

9. Ernst and Loth, *American Sexual Behavior and the Kinsey Report*, 81, 83.
10. Kinsey, et al., *Sexual Behavior in the Human Female*, 286, 332.
11. Kinsey, et al., *Sexual Behavior in the Human Female*, 416
12. Gebhard, et al., *Pregnancy, Birth and Abortion*, 62.

who induced abortions), and among later marriers, among women who aborted, it was 1.3 per woman.[13]

Despite these startling figures, the study reported that none of the thousands of women who were interviewed were harmed by rape.[14]

WAS KINSEY'S RESEARCH FRAUDULENT?

However, the Kinsey study faced criticism for its methodology. Critics pointed out that the male sample size was not representative of the general population, but was primarily composed of convicts, homosexuals, and the mentally ill. Similarly, the female sample was dominated by prostitutes, making it unrepresentative of the broader female population.[15,16]

Moreover, the impact of the fraudulent Kinsey study was far-reaching. It led to significant changes in America's legal system. Legislatures and courts relaxed state laws that had previously protected women and children, easing harsh laws against rape, adultery, child sex abuse, and incest. Additionally, criminal penalties for sex offenders were reduced in over two-thirds of U.S. states. This represented a significant shift in societal attitudes towards sexuality and the legal treatment of sexual offenses.

Further, Kinsey also based his liberal perspective on child sexual abuse on research documented in infamous tables 31- 34 in the male volume. This research detailed the systematic sexual abuse of boys ranging from 2 months to 15 years old. Despite the boys' violent reactions and crying, Kinsey concluded that they derived pleasure from being stimulated by pedophiles. Kinsey referred to the sexual responses of boys as a "climax." He observed that some boys "suffer excruciating pain and may scream if movement is

13. Gebhard, et al., *Pregnancy, Birth and Abortion*, 103.

14. Kinsey, et al., *Sexual Behavior in the Human Female*, 122.

15. Jeffrey and Ray, *A History of the American Law Institute's Model Penal Code: The Kinsey Report' Influence on "Science-Based" Legal Reform 1923–2007*, 11.

16. Cochran, et al., *Statistical Problems of the Kinsey Report*, 675, 711–16.

continued or the penis even touched will fight away from the partner." Said Kinsey, the boys may weep, faint, and scream No! "[T]hey derive definite pleasure from the situation."[17]

In Kinsey's view, what people considered rape was merely "sex play" with children especially if the age gaps were narrow. He deemed rape as essentially harmless, especially if the child gave "consent."[18] He even made a disturbing observation that an orgasm was recorded for a female infant of 4 months. Located on the campus of Indiana University, the Kinsey Institute continues to withhold the records of the Kinsey child sex data from public scrutiny.

When Kinsey's book, which included these quotes and tables, was released, no one seemed to question how this information was obtained. Paul Gebhard, co-author of Kinsey's reports, revealed that Kinsey employed trained, so-called "responsible" pedophiles for his research. They used stopwatches to record their activities.[19] In this context, rape victims were referred to as "contacts," and their screams were attributed to a "fit problem."[20]

Kinsey wrote: "It is difficult to understand why a child, except for its cultural conditioning, should be disturbed at having its genitalia touched, or disturbed at seeing the genitalia of other persons, or disturbed at even more specific sexual contacts."[21]

Kinsey's team claimed to have collected data from 18,000 individuals. However, it was later revealed that a significant portion of this data was purged. In 1971, William Simon, a senior researcher at the Kinsey Institute, admitted that 75% of the subjects interviewed by the Kinsey team were excluded from their studies.[22]

Kinsey himself was a controversial figure. Described as a "sexual psychopath" by his critics, he was seen as an amoral and unrepentant sex criminal. Despite this, he presented his research as a reflection of the sexual behaviors of average white males and

---

17. Kinsey, et al., *Sexual Behavior in the Human Male*, 160–61.
18. Kinsey, et al., *Sexual Behavior in the Human Female*, 117.
19. Reisman, *Kinsey: Crimes & Consequences*, 293.
20. Reisman, *Kinsey: Crimes & Consequences*, 155–56.
21. Kinsey, et al., *Sexual Behavior in the Human Female*, 121.
22. Reisman, *Kinsey: Crimes & Consequences*, 52.

females. However, there has never been a scientific replication of the Kinsey data, partly because of cherry-picking the data, which further casts doubt on its accuracy and reliability.

In 1977, Paul Gebhard, the director of the Kinsey Institute and co-author of Kinsey's reports, "cleaned" the data using a grant. This process resulted in a select population of subjects, approximately 87% of whom were aberrant males. This skewed sample further undermined the credibility of Kinsey's research.[23]

Kinsey's research also exhibited a clear racial bias. He excluded data collected from 934 black women, even though their experiences could have provided valuable insights into the sexual behaviors of hard-working, churchgoing families.[24] Kinsey's choice to exclude this significant group from his database has been scrutinized as an indication of his racial prejudice, which included his assumption that the black community was more "uninhibited" than their white counterparts. What, therefore, led him to eliminate the crucial segment of black college women from his database? Could it be that their responses to his inquiries were not in line with his expectations?[25]

Furthermore, Kinsey excluded all instances of homosexual incest from his report. This omission, coupled with the lack of follow-up studies to assess the long-term impact of molestation on children, has led to accusations of selective reporting and a failure to fully investigate the harm caused by sexual abuse.[26]

THE IMPACT OF KINSEY REPORTS ON THE MODEL PENAL CODE

The American Law Institute, composed of distinguished judges, lawyers, criminologists, psychiatrists, sociologists, and educators, aims to clarify and modernize the law. They introduced the

23. Reisman and Eichel, *Kinsey, Sex and Fraud: The Indoctrination of a People*, 191.
24. Kinsey, et al., *Sexual Behavior in the Human Female*, 22.
25. Reisman, *Kinsey: Crimes & Consequences*, 117.
26. Reisman, *Kinsey: Crimes & Consequences*, 158.

Model Penal Code (MPC), which significantly transformed the legal landscape, particularly regarding sex laws, heavily influenced by the controversial and fraudulent Kinsey Report. The initiative was funded by the Rockefeller Foundation, which provided momentum to write the MPC. Four disciples of Kinsey—Wechsler, Schwartz, Ploscowe, and Tappan—were instrumental in creating the 1955 MPC sex offenses draft.

The Kinsey report suggested that existing laws needed to be revised to reflect the social norms that it claimed to uncover. Kinsey's assertion that 95% of men were sex offenders implied that the laws were broken, and enforcement was impossible. This sentiment resonated with the authors of the MPC, who sought to reduce or eliminate the over 50 prohibitions from state law. Morris Ernst, in his 1948 book, "American Sexual Behavior and the Kinsey Report," advocated for the elimination or reduction of over 50 sex offenses.[27] The MPC, with all 197 footnotes in the "Sex Offenses" section cites Kinsey's work. Kinsey's studies suggested that acts such as fornication, adultery, rape, sodomy, bestiality, and child sex abuse were "normal" and harmless private sexual behaviors.[28] Kinsey argued that sodomy, being a private act, was so prevalent (37% of the population in the 1940s-50s) that enforcing laws against it was impractical.[29] Kinsey also contended that rape was not a grave issue unless significant force was involved.[30] He dismissed child molestation as non-existent, asserting that children are sexual and erotic beings from birth.[31] He believed that many children could benefit from sexual interactions with adults, despite parental objections that are rooted in custom or moral reasons. Hence, if incest and child rape were largely harmless, then a call to parole of all offenders was the result. For these reasons, the MPC trivialized all sex crimes, with Kinsey being cited as the sole authority for defining these acts as "normal" human sexual behavior.

27. Ernst and Loth, *American Sexual Behavior and the Kinsey Report*, 127.
28. Reisman, *Kinsey: Crimes & Consequences*, 204.
29. Kinsey, et al., *Sexual Behavior in the Human Male*, 638–41.
30. Reisman, *Sexual Sabotage*, 35.
31. Kinsey, et al., *Sexual Behavior in the Human Male*, 178.

The 1955 draft was distributed to all states, with crime commissions quoting Kinsey, stressing the importance of aligning their laws with his findings. The adoption of the MPC began in Wisconsin, in 1956, and nearly all state legislatures subsequently adopted all or part of the MPC. This marked a significant departure from previous laws and established a new legal framework for dealing with sex offenses.

Kinsey's outreach extended also to training psychiatric experts, federal, state, and local law enforcement, courts and parole boards, law schools and journals, and private, public, and parochial education. Kinsey's fraudulent research emphasized the importance of professional sex education to teach children the "facts" about sex further emphasizing the shift towards the so-called scientific approach to sexuality.

This extensive influence led to the displacement of the long-standing authority of the common law based on revealed and eternal laws to an evolutionary and relativistic law based on the fraudulent "sex science authority." Or we can say a shift from law order to lawyer order, or rule by elites. A significant portion of the MPC is structured in a manner that diminishes the authority of juries to adjudicate while amplifying the influence of experts. This is achieved through expert testimonies, which guide the application of specific subclassifications and penalties.[32] Richard Kuh, a prosecutor from New York states:

> If the draftsmen [ALI/MPC] wish to force trial judges to stop and puzzle over abstruse wording, that discipline can do no harm. But the trouble is that the draftsmen are here engaged in linguistic embroidery to which lay jurors would inevitably be exposed. This worries me . . . . But awkward phrases and shrouded concepts bother me; for instructions in the law—jury charges—are delivered to jurors orally, and may go on for hours. Furthermore, they may contain a variety of precepts with which the jurors have never before had to deal, and concerning which, if

---

32. Bose, *Law Order Vs. Lawyer Order: Analyzing the Development of Jury Independence*, 287.

a verdict is to be reached, the jurors must all end up as of one mind, convinced beyond a reasonable doubt.[33]

However, their work overlooked the societal implications of these acts, such as venereal diseases, the blight of prostitution and pornography, child abuse, unintended pregnancies, drug and alcohol abuse, abortion, and numerous other negative externalities.

The MPC's influence extended to the judiciary, with historian David Allyn reporting that it directly informed two early major Supreme Court decisions in a contradictory way: *Roth v. United States* 354 U.S. 476 (1957), and *Griswold v. Connecticut*, 381 U.S. 479 (1965). He states that the Kinsey studies:

> [P]layed a critical role in the mid-century privatization of morality. In the post-WWII era, experts abandoned the concept of "public morals," a concept which had underpinned the social control of American sexuality from the 1870's onward. In the 1950's and 60's, however, sexual morality was privatized, and the state-controlled, highly regulated moral economy of the past gave way to a new, "deregulated" moral market.... This theoretical opposition [between private and public sexual expression] allowed the Supreme Court to produce two seemingly contradictory lines of argument in *Roth v. The United States* (1957) and *Griswold v. Connecticut* (1965). The first upheld the criminality of pornography while the second established the sexual rights of married couples. Both cases drew on the American Law Institute's model penal code's distinction between public and private sexual expression, which, in turn, drew on the work of Alfred Kinsey.[34]

THE IMPACT OF KINSEY IN THE LEGAL ARENA

By the year 1950, the fraudulent Kinsey Report was revolutionary on a broad scale. This transformation was recognized by the Dean

---

33. Kuh, *A Prosecutor Considers the Model Penal Code*, 622.

34. Allyn, *Private Acts/Public Policy: Alfred Kinsey, the American Law Institute and the Privatization of American Sexual Morality*, 406.

of Indiana Law School in an article published in the Illinois Law Review, where he underscored the substantial influence of Kinsey's report on the legal field. He states:

> The principal impact of the Kinsey Report will be at the level of the administration of the law. It will provide the statistical support which police officers, prosecutors, judges, probation officers and superintendents of penal institutions need for judging individual cases.
> Officials will read it. Defense counsel will cite it. *Even when not offered* into evidence, it will condition official action. Psychiatrists, psychologists, penologists, juvenile and probation officers ... they will use the data and their professional advice will be heeded by the judge. Here the Report will control many decisions and dictate the disposition and treatment of many offenders.[35]

Further, even if there is a public outcry with a decision and data must be dismissed, social scientists need to think in geologic time when trying to implement the findings of the fraudulent Kinsey Report.

In 1953, Hugh Hefner, an ardent follower of Kinsey, instigated a considerable change in societal viewpoints. He published the Playboy magazine. Hefner brought Kinsey's theories out of the academic closet into the public eye, especially among university students. This resulted in a shift with future societal leaders, who started to deviate from the conventional values of marital affection and safeguarding of wife and children. Instead, they began to embrace the notion of recreational sex.[36]

Slovenko and Phillips, authors from Tulane University School of Law and School of Medicine, felt that laws dealing with sexual crimes, rather than addressing them, exacerbated the issue. Further, individual freedoms are restricted unnecessarily. Using the Kinsey studies as the foundation, the authors studied various sex crime laws, including the rape of children by "helpless" aged men and women. They channeled Kinsey's ideas that children are sexual beings when they wrote:

---

35. Horack, *Sex Offenses and Scientific Investigation*, 156, 58.
36. Reisman, *Sexual Sabotage*, 104–05.

Even at the age of four or five, [her] *seductiveness may be so powerful* as to overwhelm the adult into committing the offense. The affair is therefore not always the result of the adult's aggression; often the young female is the initiator and seducer (italics added).[37]

In an unauthored note in the Georgia Law Review, the authors first cited Kinsey that most males were sex criminals and state that it was absurd to enforce "most of our sex laws, not to mention the impossibility of such enforcement, should be obvious, even to the most prudish Neo-Puritans." Further, they noted that pedophilia/child molestation is a "relatively minor" crime. And that further, various excuses were made by the authors for such offenders such as social pressures, physical needs, marital difficulties, and so on.[38]

The consequence of treating child molestation lightly and advocating for it was the lightening of punishments for child predators. In 1990, the American Bar Association (ABA) reported that the vast majority of individuals convicted of child molestation were granted parole and did not serve any time in prison. Furthermore, these offenders were likely to receive taxpayer-funded treatment for their "sexual orientation" towards children. While under probation these individuals were less likely to reoffend, after probation, it was not clear. In one study, 89% were required to go for treatment as part of probation requirements.[39]

In 1998, U.S. Supreme Court Associate Justice Stephen Breyer looked at the role of science in various forms of law, "[L]aw cases can turn almost entirely on an understanding of the underlying technical or scientific subject matter." While he was here particularly talking about patent laws, it can be applied to sex laws also. He further states that "science itself may be highly uncertain and controversial with respect to many of the matters that come before

---

37. Slovenko and Phillips, *Psychosexuality and the Criminal Law*, 809.

38. *Pedophilia, Exhibitionism, and Voyeurism: Legal Problems in the Deviant Society*, 150.

39. *The Probation Response to Child Sexual Abuse Offenders: How Is It Working?*, 1, 7.

the courts." But what if the science is fraudulent?[40] The impact of the fraudulent Kinsey reports on Supreme Court cases did unfortunately occur in many additional cases.

As stated earlier, two decisions by the Supreme Court that used Kinsey's fraudulent science including *Roth v. the United States* represented a distinct effort to control public sexual behavior. The court ruled that obscenity was beyond the First Amendment's rights to free speech and press. Whereas *Griswold v. Connecticut* was a rejection of state interference in private sexual conduct. The court ruled against the anti-contraception statute due to notions of privacy surrounding marriage relationships. The right to privacy though not explicitly stated in the constitution, was found in the penumbra of other constitutional provisions like in the Third, Fourth, Fifth, and Ninth Amendments.[41] The Griswold decision eventually led to the *Eisenstadt v. Baird*, 405 U.S. 438 (1972) decision extending the right to privacy to unmarried couples, and, in 1973, to the *Roe v. Wade*, 410 U.S. 113 (1973), and *Doe v. Bolton*, 410 U.S. 179 (1973) decisions. In the latter two cases, the Supreme Court said that the right to privacy includes abortion, and abortion was theoretically legal for any reason till full term.

A few decades later, *Lawrence v. Texas*, 539 U.S. 558 (2003), addressed sodomy laws by invalidating them in several states. It drew substantial influence from Alfred Kinsey's work and the Model Penal Code (MPC). The verdict was entirely grounded in Kinsey's expertise in the field. Justice Kennedy invoked the 1955 MPC in his reasoning, and allusions to the history of homosexuality were made, primarily sourcing from Kinsey's research. Justice Scalia, however, voiced apprehensions about the potential ramifications of this ruling. He cautioned that it might incite challenges to the sanctity of marriage, potentially paving the way for practices like polygamy, bestiality, and sadism. Scalia's warning came true with the *Obergefell v. Hodges* 576 U.S. 644 (2015)

---

40. Breyer, *The Interdependence of Science and Law*, 537.

41. Hull and Hoffer, *Roe V. Wade: The Abortion Rights Controversy in American History*, 84.

decision, which redefined marriage qualitatively to now include two women or two men.[42]

THE INFLUENCE OF KINSEY ON SCHOOLS

Another impact of the Kinsey studies was to push sexually explicit material on school children as educational tools. Mary Calderone, Planned Parenthood's medical director, became founder and Director of SIECUS, the Sex Information and Education Council of the U.S. Mary Calderone, wrote of the role of SIECUS:

> Thus we applied and were approved for a highly important grant from the National Institute for Mental Health that was designed to implement a planned role for SIECUS to become the primary data base for the area of education for sexuality.[43]

SIECUS supports the use of sexually pornographic materials (whether "visual, printed, or online") for school children as a valuable resource for a healthy understanding of sexuality among students.[44]

Kinsey's impact was also felt among Christian educators. Paul Cameron held a PhD and was an early follower of Kinsey's teachings, as well as a prominent figure in Christian sexology education. He served as a lecturer and educator at the Fuller Theological Seminary from 1976 to 1979. In 1978, Cameron authored a book titled "Sexual Gradualism." This work suggested a progressive approach to teenage sexuality. Cameron advised parents to provide a private space, complete with amenities like a bathroom, a TV, and snacks for their teenagers. This setup was intended to allow teenagers to explore their sexuality gradually and without fear of intrusion.

Dr. Cameron's "gradualism," moved from "breast fondling" to "exploration of genitals" to "total nudity" and "oral sex" as they

---

42. Reisman and Mcalister, *Nearly 60 Years after His Death, Alfred Kinsey's Pansexual Worldview Takes Root in Marriage Decisions*, 48–52.

43. Calderone, *Siecus Report*, 6.

44. *Siecus Report*, 15.

go through their teen years. Sexual intercourse was to be reserved for marriage. His approach was certainly not Christian, but rather an attempt to merge Kinsey's fraudulent findings with Christian abstinence.[45]

Lenore Buth, a Christian author, in her book *How to Talk Confidently to Your Child About Sex*, writes that children are sexual at birth.

> It may be surprising to realize that our children are sexual beings from birth. For instance, a parent changing a male infant's diaper may accidentally stimulate the child and be shocked to realize the child is having an erection. Similarly, researchers tell us that baby girls have vaginal lubrication regularly. In fact, a little girl being bounced on her parent's knee may feel pleasant sensations and begin to make natural pelvic thrust movements.[46]

Buth's comment indicates that she is a "theological expert" for Kinsey and his pedophile followers. Numerous Christian and secular "abstinence" education programs have been found in the K-12 arena providing a Christian cover for Kinsey.

Before the Kinsey era, it was even illegal to show sexually explicit images to minors in all cases, even for medical purposes like demonstrating venereal diseases. Considering their heterogeneous backgrounds and emotional stability, there is no scientific evidence supporting the exposure of children to sexual content through images or probing questions. However, current obscenity laws even permit the display of explicit content to minors in educational institutions like libraries and schools.

CONCLUSION

The research team led by Kinsey and the subjects they studied have been a topic of intense debate and scrutiny. The team's fraudulent

---

45 Cameron, *Sexual Gradualism: A Solution to the Sexual Dilemma of Teen-Agers and Young Adults*, 7,24,32.

46. Buth, *How to Talk Confidently to Your Child About Sex*, 23.

findings have had a profound impact on our legal and educational systems. Further, as society becomes sexually free, Unwin suggests that economic collapse is not far behind. The methods employed by Kinsey's team and the selective nature of his data have raised serious ethical and methodological concerns. Ultimately, if Kinsey's sexology is debunked, it would have a domino effect on various avenues and related programs.[47] In the next chapter, we will quantify the impact of Kinsey by tracking the changes to sex laws that occurred. Quantifying the impact will allow for rigorous empirical analysis.

---

47. Interestingly, it was only in 2023, that the Indiana state legislature decided to not allocate any state monies for the Kinsey Institute. https://www.heraldtimesonline.com/story/news/2023/04/28/kinsey-institute-no-longer-to-have-state-dollars-after-budget-adoption/70163039007/ (accessed September 5, 2024).

4

Assessing Sexual Freedom across the 50 States

1960 to 2010

Feler Bose & Ari Kornelis

...the conduct of life is to so large an extent determined by the existing legal institutions, that an understanding of the legal system must give you a clearer view of human affairs in their manifold relations, and must aid you in comprehending the conditions, and institutions by which you are surrounded.[1]

LOUIS D. BRANDEIS, FORMER ASSOCIATE JUSTICE AT THE U.S. SUPREME COURT

AS WE LEARNED IN the last chapter, the fraudulent Kinsey studies had a major impact on the changing of the state laws in the United States. In this chapter, we will codify the change that has happened

---

1. Baker, *Brandeis and Frankfurter: A Dual Biography*, 29.

over fifty-one years. Scholars have not completed serious quantitative work on the topic of sexual freedom. Numerous scholars and think tanks have spent resources measuring economic freedom, political freedom, and other freedoms using indexes in either the 50 U.S. States or around the world.[2] Some of the indexes include the Drug Freedom Index,[3] Gun Rights Index,[4] and the Index of Economic Freedom.[5] Ruger and Sorens developed a comprehensive Index of Personal and Economic Freedom for the 50 US states, but their attention to sexual freedom is limited to primarily homosexual marriage and at times the prostitution variable and is available only for a few years.[6] There continues to be a significant gap in the existing freedom index literature. There is no index measuring sexual freedom.

This chapter presents a main Sexual Freedom Index measuring median voter preferences and discusses the lived freedom index. These indexes compare the various degrees of permissiveness toward sexual and extra marital activity in the 50 U.S. States. Further, once sexual freedom is quantified, it allows for hypothesis testing. The scope of this chapter is confined to a presentation of all the Indexes, a basic analysis of the apparent trends in the data, and deals with the issue of norms, laws, and dead letter laws.

BOUNDARIES OF THE SEXUAL FREEDOM INDEX (SFI)

The creation of any index is both an art and a science. All indexes need a starting point for coding the variables. We define minimum sexual freedom when laws recognize only two persons (quantitative) male and female (qualitative) in marriage as the legal sexual

---

2. For example, the Fraser Institute tracks economic freedom in the world (http://www.freetheworld.com/).

3. Accessed at http://www.freeexistence.org/drugindex.html on 3/15/14.

4. Accessed at http://www.freeexistence.org/gunindex.html on 3/15/14.

5. Accessed at http://www.heritage.org/index/ on 9/5/24.

6. Accessed at http://freedominthe50states.org on 9/5/24. The years that are scored include 2001, 2007, 2009, 2011, 2013, 2016, 2018, 2021, and 2023.

arrangement.[7] Historically, both family law and criminal law have supported limiting sexual activity to the realm of marriage to protect the sanctity of marriage.[8] Following this understanding, we used fifteen variables and divided them into two categories: laws that define and protect traditional marriage that is acceptable, and laws that penalize sexual behaviors outside of marriage that are deemed unacceptable. The set of variables was selected with the intention that the overall index would present a comprehensive understanding of each state's legal limitations on sexual and marital behavior.[9] Table 4-1 shows the variables that were used for the index creation and the two categories that they fall under allowing for the creation of subindexes.

Table 4-1: Variables used for developing the Sexual Freedom Index and the category of each variable.

Sex Crimes Freedom sub-Index	Bestiality, Abortion, Sodomy, Fornication, Pimp laws, Prostitution laws, and Age of Consent.
Marriage Protection Freedom sub-Index	Adultery, Homosexual marriage and its recognition, Polygamy, Divorce, Cohabitation, Miscegenation, and Marry close blood.

In a working paper, Bose began a discussion of this material using an initial single-year sample of sexual freedom data from 2010.[10] However, in this chapter, we have traced state laws regulating sexuality back to 1960 using mainly legal archives hosted by

---

7. Two of the variables do deviate from this definition. They are the miscegenation laws and marrying close blood.

8. Murray, *Strange Bedfellows: Criminal Law, Family Law and the Legal Construction of Intimate Life*, 1257.

9. Some indexes like the social capital index are based on 14 variables and the natural amenities index uses only a handful of categories. Among, economic freedom indexes, the publication from American Legislative Exchange Council uses 15 fiscal and regulatory variables to provide state rankings, the Fraser Institute index only uses 10 variables and the Mercatus Center index uses dozens of variables.

10. Bose, *License to Sin: The Politics and Opportunity Cost of Sexual Freedom*, 1–41.

LexisNexis Academic and HeinOnline,[11] in coordination with numerous books (e.g., Pascoe for miscegenation[12]) journal articles, court cases, and websites.[13] We chose 1960 as the starting year since the most comprehensive state-level databases usually start from this year e.g., Richard Fording's ideology measures.[14]

The variables included are primarily "victimless crimes."[15,16] Sexual crimes with victims or crimes that involve non-consenting persons were not included in the Sexual Freedom Index (SFI). These include crimes such as rape and sexual assault. Sexual harassment, crimes related to lewdness or indecent exposure, have also been excluded because they involve non-consenting persons. Censorship and pornography laws are also excluded from the SFI. Censorship law is distinct from any of the variables included in the SFI and potentially difficult to code. While additional variables could have been chosen, there were diminishing marginal returns to adding variables.

Figure 4-1 labeled 'Total Index Minus Selected Variables' shows the trajectory of the total SFI and compares them with the total SFI minus two separate variables that have the most unique trajectories. Freedom to commit sodomy increases sharply, during the 1970s and more gradually later. Freedom for bestiality increased during the 1970s and then decreased steadily afterward. Despite the difference between the trajectories of each variable,

11. Occasionally we used Westlaw.

12. Pascoe, *What Comes Naturally: Miscegenation Law and the Making of Race in America*, 1–416.

13. For bestiality: https://www.animallaw.info/articles/ovuszoophilia.htm (accessed multiple dates 2013–2017).

14. http://rcfording.wordpress.com/state-ideology-data/ (accessed 9/6/2024).

15. "Victimless crimes" are illegal activities that do not directly harm another person or property. In the area of sexuality, it is usually tied to consensual activities. F.A. Hayek believes that such acts should not concern a judge. Hayek, *Law, Legislation and Liberty, Volume 1 : Rules and Order*, 101.

16. From a Christian perspective, there is no such thing as "victimless crimes." As every person "who entices another to sin is bringing that person under God's negative sanctions . . . God therefore threatens the whole community for its failure to impose civil sanctions against such crimes." North, *Victim's Rights: The Biblical View of Civil Justice*, 225.

removing any variable from the total index does little to adjust the overall trajectory of the sexual freedom index. Qualitatively nothing changes, indicating our index is robust and adding additional variables is not necessary.

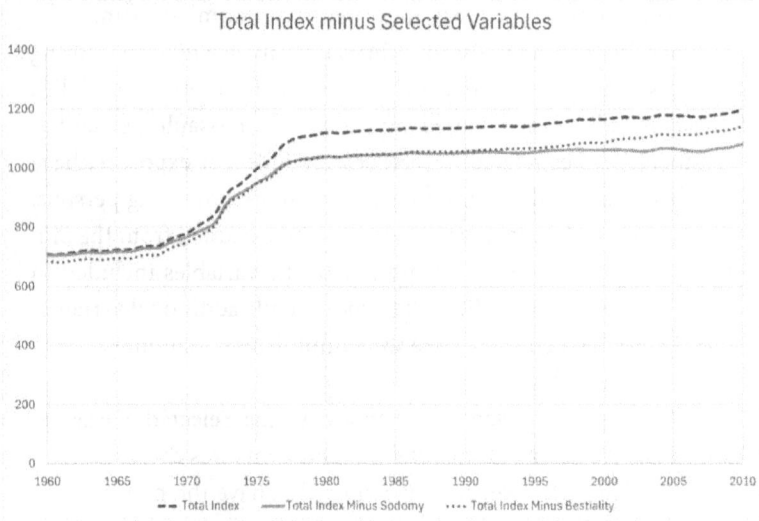

Figure 4-1: Taking the total Sexual Freedom Index and subtracting the 2 variables showing the most variation shows that qualitatively the index doesn't change much.

DETAILS OF THE CODING METHOD FOR THE SFI

The data is coded annually for each of the fifty U.S. states from 1960-2010 for a total of 51 years. Thus, each of the fifteen variables has 2,550 state years, for a total of 38,250 data points. The data was coded on a four-point scale (0, 1, 2, 3). In the final index, each of the fifteen variables is given equal weight and added to create an SFI value for each of the 2,550 state years. Researchers have also used other advanced techniques such as Principal Component Analysis to create indexes.[17] The advantage of an

17. Rupasingha, et al., *The Production of Social Capital in U.S. Counties*,

equal weight index is that other researchers can add or subtract variables to create their own SFI. With this data, trends can be observed across time, within individual states, between numerous states, and groups of states.

The four-point scale was chosen to establish a greater degree of nuance than would be achievable with a binary legal/illegal method. A value of zero reflects the lowest possible amount of freedom, and a three represents the greatest amount of freedom. The variables that are penalized under criminal law were relatively unambiguous in coding. The variables were coded with a zero if, in a given state year, the behavior was punishable as a felony. The variable would be coded with a one if the behavior is punishable as a misdemeanor, a two either if the behavior is punished as a petty crime, (minimal fine, no jail time), or if it is a misdemeanor in certain parts of the state and not others. A petty offense is usually not considered a crime.[18] Finally, a behavior that is not punishable in a given state year would receive a three.

Unfortunately, all states do not employ a uniform definition of a felony. Some states do not use felony misdemeanor classifications at all. As noted by Logan, Stellwagen, and Langen "two jurisdictions (Maine and New Jersey) do not use the term (felony) to classify their criminal offenses, and six others offer no explicit definition of the term, even though they use it as a criminal designation."[19] To address this ambiguity, we employ a distinction used in the criminal law literature to standardize these labels and avoid variance between states. For this chapter, a felony is any crime punishable by a minimum sentence of at least one year of jail time.[20] Also presented by the Bureau of Justice Statistics is a list of each state's definition of felony. A plurality of nineteen states defines a felony as a crime punishable by at least one year in prison. Subsequently, a misdemeanor is any crime punishable by

---

83–101.

18. Torcia, *Wharton's Criminal Law 15th Edition*, 18.

19. Logan, et al., *Felony Laws of the 50 States and the District of Columbia, 1986*, v.

20. Podgor, et al., *Mastering Criminal Law*, 11.

a minimum sentence of less than one year of jail time. Finally, a petty crime is any crime not punishable by jail time. Typically, the penalty for a petty crime is a small fine.[21] Further, if something was a crime, we focused on the punishment received during the first offense, not the punishment for subsequent offenses. Further, the coding avoided any focus on minors.

Certain variables, including many that fall under family law, could not be coded using a method tied to the felony/misdemeanor/petty crime distinctions. For each variable, a set of distinctions was designed to clarify the coding process and to allow for replication. This element of creative interpretation leads some to refer to coding as both an art and a science.[22] Many of the variables in the second category (relationships prevented to protect marriage) are prohibited in family or marriage law but do not carry criminal penalties. For these variables, it was necessary to adjust the coding method to consider the relative legal obstacles to obtaining legal recognition of certain relationships.

In measuring divorce, for example, we measured the relative obstacles to nullifying a marriage in each state year. Unilateral (no-fault) divorce is the easiest and thus most free form of divorce. So, states that allow for unilateral divorce are the freest concerning divorce law. States requiring mutual consent are the next most free, followed by states that allow divorce only after evidence has been given of certain faults. When measuring the barriers to the attainment of divorce, the work of Malcolm Gold whose working paper was extremely valuable.[23]

---

21. Logan, et al., *Felony Laws of the 50 States and the District of Columbia, 1986*, vii ff.

22. Bose, *License to Sin: The Politics and Opportunity Cost of Sexual Freedom*, 8.

23. Gold, *Divorce and Divorce Reform: A Reconciliation of Results at Odds*, 1–59.

Table 4–2: Coding method used for creating the Sexual Freedom Indexes.

Policy	0: Least Free	1	2	3: Most Free
General Adultery, Prostitution (pimps and prostitutes), Bestiality, Fornication, Cohabitation, Sodomy, Polygamy, Miscegenation	Felony	Misdemeanor	Misdemeanor in limited regions/ Petty Crime	Not a Crime
Age of Consent (Minimum age that one may consent to legal sexual activity)	19 and up	17, 18	15, 16	14 and under
Close Blood Marriage	Cousin Marriage is prohibited in all circumstances.	Cousin Marriage is allowed with proof of infertility or between persons over the age of 50		Cousin Marriage is allowed without reservations.
Divorce (requirements for legal divorce)	Not routinely allowed	Fault	Mutual Consent/ No Fault	None (Unilateral)
Homosexual Marriage	Prohibited	Civil Unions		Allowed
Recognition of other state's Homosexual Marriage	No by amendment	No by statue		Yes
Abortion (Legality of Abortions in the absence of *Roe v. Wade*)	Prohibited			Allowed

We operationalized marrying close blood as the marriage of one's first cousin. Virtually all states prohibit marriage by people of closer relation than first cousins. There is less consensus on the legality of first-cousin marriage. I considered the states where it is either fully legal or fully illegal as the most and least free respectively. Some states allow cousin marriage under certain limited circumstances. Several states allow marriage of first cousins between persons over 50, or between a couple either of whom has been proven to be infertile. These states were coded as one for somewhat free.

We used a simple coding scheme for abortion. We asked the question of what the status of abortion would be in the absence of *Roe v. Wade* (410 U.S. 113) (hereafter referred to as *Roe v. Wade*). If it was prohibited, we coded the state as least free, if allowed, it was coded as most free.

It is important to clarify the definitions of fornication and cohabitation used for this project. In many states, these laws are linked. Additionally, many states have laws that use the word fornication but include additional context that implies cohabitation. For this chapter, fornication is a single sexual act between unmarried persons. Cohabitation is the known repeated sexual conduct of unmarried persons living together. Thus, laws that refer to persons "living in an open state of fornication" were coded under the cohabitation variable and not under the fornication variable. For an outline of the coding method used for each variable see Table 4–2.

NORMS, LAWS, DEAD LETTER LAWS, AND INDEXES

One of the issues that comes up when coding sexual freedom is the issue of dead letter laws. Laws that are in the books, but seemingly not enforced. This section deals with norms, laws, dead letter laws, and the creation of our indexes.

Many laws suffer from the mobility effect of criminal penalties. Penalties seem to be relatively more responsive to desired increases from voters than desired decreases. Penalties for undesirable behaviors will increase when critical numbers desire such a change within a constituency. However, when a constituency no longer desires a penalty, the enforcement institutions will often cease to enforce the penalties for the behavior and render the statute effectively null. When this occurs, the issue is unlikely to enter the legislative agenda because those who are opposed to the penalty are content with the lack of enforcement. The enforcing institution has the autonomy to neglect to enforce an unpopular penalty. However, the institution does not have the autonomy to enforce a penalty more stringent than that defined in the statutory code. Therefore, the legislature is more responsive to desires for increased penalties than to desires for decreased penalties. For example, Idaho's constitution disenfranchised those who practiced polygamy, or even supported organizations that encouraged polygamy. It was seen as a way to strip Mormons of the right to vote. Only in 1982, almost 100 years after the Mormon Church ended support for Polygamy, was the language finally removed, and that too, even about a third of the voters wanted to keep the ban.[24]

Additionally, variables such as cohabitation and adultery, while *de jure* illegal in some states are it seems *de facto* not strictly enforced by the states. However, there are many instances where cohabitation laws are indirectly enforced. For example, cohabitation laws come into play in child custody disputes and divorce cases. In *Muller v. Muller* (711 N.W.2d 329 (2006) 474 Mich. 1074) a circuit court in Michigan had ordered that "neither party shall have an unrelated member of the opposite sex overnight while having parenting time with the minor children," while this decision was appealed to the Supreme Court of Michigan, the higher court did not reverse the decision. We coded laws based on what was in the books, not whether it was prosecuted. Further, because court cases in the U.S. are only recorded when a case is appealed occasional cohabitation and adultery cases may be dealt with by the courts[25] but because it is not recorded it is unclear how many cases are litigated.

24. Newsmax, *Idaho's Gay Marriage Ban Remains in State Constitution*, paragraphs 13, 14.

25. Coleman, *Who's Been Sleeping in My Bed? You and Me, and the State Makes Three*, 399–400.

This research is relevant to a larger discussion about the relationship between law and social norms. Strong social norms create pressures that constrain the behavior of individuals. The threat of social ostracism and shame are powerful forces for social conformity. In a common law system, the law is expected to reflect social norms. "According to an old principle in jurisprudence, judges must discover common law in social norms rather than invent law in light of their own preferences."[26] The common law was also seen as being discovered in the natural and moral law as Blackstone understood it.[27] The law then acts as a supplement to the private pressures that emerge from social norms and moral law.

Private enforcement and state enforcement typically complement each other. The cooperation of citizens with officials increases the effectiveness of state enforcement and lowers its costs; the backing of state officials increases the effectiveness of private enforcement and lowers its risks. Conversely, laws that are inconsistent with social norms are perceived as irrelevant or unjust by many citizens, who then are reluctant to help the state detect and punish individuals who break such laws.[28]

There is some controversy as to whether laws shape social norms. The evidence shows that education, culture, religion, and socialization shape social norms and laws on the other hand probably do not. Posner explains that lawyers think that the law is potentially significant as a shaper (not just an enforcer) of norms. "The evidence for this conjecture is weak, and against it can be cited evidence that subgroups will often go their own way, adhering to norms that serve their special needs but violate the applicable legal norms, which may have been created without consideration for those needs."[29] Shavell suggests that laws can also affect moral

---

26. Cooter, *The Rule of State Law and the Rule-of-Law State: Economic Analysis of the Legal Foundations of Development*, 205.

27. Bose, *Law Order Vs. Lawyer Order: Analyzing the Development of Jury Independence*, 10–12.

28. Cooter, *The Rule of State Law and the Rule-of-Law State: Economic Analysis of the Legal Foundations of Development*, 201ff.

29. Posner, *Social Norms and the Law; an Economic Approach*, 368.

beliefs and further that it is possible to have laws that counter the moral rule held by a majority if a group with political power can override those wishes.[30] For this reason, laws are then also a reflection of interest groups' preferences more so than social norms. Legal pressure can also result in individuals misrepresenting their genuine position "under perceived social pressures" which has been called preference falsification.[31] One paper suggests that legal recognition of homosexual relationships resulted in increased support among individuals for sexual minorities, i.e., that laws can shape attitudes and morality.[32]

When the laws support the social norms, they are more likely to be obeyed. When the laws conflict with the social norms, they are more likely to be disobeyed and under-enforced. So, social norms create significant social pressure, and they do not emerge from the law. Thus, measuring law is an imperfect method for measuring freedom. When measuring political freedom, it is important to recognize that private enforcement of social norms reduces human freedom regardless of state enforcement. Posner notes that "norm internalization reduces human freedom, viewed functionally in terms of scope of choice rather than formalistically as freedom from legal constraints."[33] An accurate measure of freedom must consider social norms rather than the law alone. To achieve a better proxy of social norms, it is important to aim measurements toward smaller constituencies, and more democratic processes. A U.S. Supreme Court decision may not accurately reflect social norms because the Supreme Court is removed from any democratic process.

The primary SFI is directed at state-level constituencies to more accurately reflect differences in social norms or median voter preferences as they vary between states. Although Supreme Court

30. Shavell, *Law Versus Morality as Regulators of Conduct*, 254–55.

31. Kuran, *Private Truths, Public Lies: The Social Consequences of Preference Falsification*, 3.

32. Aksoy, et al., *Do Laws Shape Attitudes? Evidence from Same-Sex Relationship Recognition Policies in Europe*, 1.

33. Posner, *Social Norms and the Law; an Economic Approach*, 367.

decisions certainly influence state legislatures, our main index focuses on what is written in state laws. Although a Supreme Court decision may render a statute null, the SFI will not change values until the state legislature changes the law. We consider only decisions made within the state. The SFI does reflect the decisions of state courts because state courts more closely reflect the preferences of the state voters than the federal courts. *Roe v. Wade* provides an excellent example of conflicting desires between states and the federal courts. Numerous states have instituted 'trigger laws' that would immediately recriminalize abortions if the Supreme Court were to overturn *Roe v. Wade*.[34,35] State politicians are more responsive to the median voter preferences within their state than the federal courts. It is important to consider these complexities because they more closely reflect actual voter preferences. Voter preferences, in turn, more closely reflect the prevailing social norms.

In the area of interracial marriage, Alabama provides a revealing case study. In 2000, Alabama had a ballot measure to repeal an amendment in its constitution banning interracial marriage. The repeal passed with 59% of the vote. This indicates that social norms in Alabama took a long time to change.[36]

It is also important to note that laws lag behind social norms. Certain behaviors may be unacceptable under the prevailing social norms, but they may not become penalized in state law until it is apparent that the social norms are not sufficient for preventing breaches of the standard. This occurred in the 1800s with the issue of abortion where the Southern states in the U.S. did not have abortion laws because social norms were sufficiently strong to discourage abortions, whereas the Northeastern states did.[37]

---

34. Smock, *What If Roe Fell? The State-by-State Consequences of Overturning Roe V. Wade*, 13.

35. With the recent *Dobbs v. Jackson Women's Health Organization* (597 U.S. _2022) decision that overturned Roe v. Wade, many trigger laws have come into effect and some are being actively litigated.

36. http://ballotpedia.org/wiki/index.php/Alabama_Interracial_Marriage,_Amendment_2_%282000%29 (accessed April 18, 2013).

37. Olasky, *Abortion Rites: A Social History of Abortion in America*, 102.

SEXUAL FREEDOM INDEXES: MEDIAN VOTER PREFERRED VS. LIVED FREEDOM

In this chapter, we will discuss two different Sexual Freedom Indexes. The main Sexual Freedom Index tracks the preference of the median voter/social norms in the state. To do this, we keep track of what the law says to reflect the preferences of the median voter. The second Sexual Freedom Index focuses on what is allowed or lived sexual freedom. For the latter index, we consider the decisions of the U.S. Supreme Court. If the U.S. Supreme Court declares a variable legal, then it is considered legal in that state. The laws for all intents and purposes cannot be and are not enforced regardless of the preferences of the median voter. Since the Lived Freedom Index is responsive to Supreme Court decisions, a spike in freedom will occur in 1967 for miscegenation (*Loving v. Virginia*, 388 U.S. 1), 1973 for abortion (*Roe v. Wade*, 410 U.S. 113), and 2003 for sodomy (*Lawrence v. Texas*, 539 U.S. 558). For the main Sexual Freedom Index, where the median voter preferences are key, it won't be responsive to Supreme Court decisions, so the changes in miscegenation, abortion, and sodomy laws change gradually over time. Figure 4–2 shows the two different indexes.

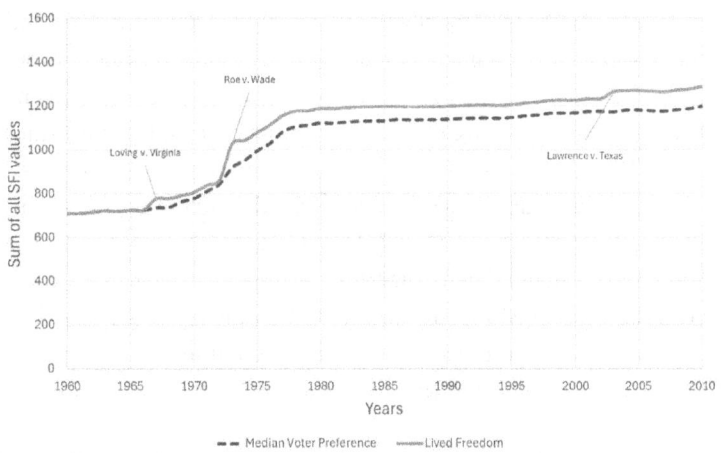

Figure 4–2: Lived freedom vs. median voter preferred Sexual Freedom Index. Three U.S. Supreme Court cases impact the Lived freedom index creating jumps in the Lived freedom index.

ANALYSIS OF RESULTS OVER 51 YEARS

The data demonstrate a dramatic increase in sexual freedom within the measured period. There are several important trends to note. There is a general trend toward greater sexual freedom, however, this trend has not been steady over time. There was a watershed period of dramatic change during the 1970s. Secondly, the data defies a conclusive theory of regional convergence, although mild regional cohesion may be observed. The West Coast and Northeast are fairly congruous in higher levels of freedom after the 1970s.

When considering the differences between the final and initial SFI values, forty-nine states are freer in 2010 than they were in 1960. Michigan is the only state that is equally sexually free in 2010 as in 1960. Other than Michigan, the states that have changed the least include North Carolina (2 points), South Dakota (2 points), Illinois (3 points), and Oklahoma (3 points). The states that have increased the most include (Connecticut 20 points), Maine (19 points), Iowa (18 points), Wyoming (17 points), and Texas (17 points). The shift toward increasing sexual freedom is powerful in its inclusiveness. Nearly all states have become freer, and no state has become less free.

When considering the amount of change in SFI values by decade, 70% of the total change that occurred between 1960 and 2010 occurred during the 1970s.[38] The next most tumultuous decade is the 1960s with 14% of the total change. The average state has become increasingly sexually free by 9.76 SFI points since 1960. The average change in the 1970s alone was 6.84 SFI points.

The dramatic change that occurred during the 1970s was influenced mainly by the Model Penal Code (MPC). The MPC is a set of recommended penal statutes created by the legal elites at the American Law Institute and was based on the fraudulent work of Alfred Kinsey (see last chapter).[39] Kinsey found that Americans were sexually active and that the laws which protected traditional

---

38. This is calculated as the total positive change in SFI values in the 1970s as a percent of total positive change in the SFI between 1960 and 2010.

39. Reisman, *Sexual Sabotage*, 78–79.

marriage did not reflect social norms, they needed to be changed including those tied to rape.

Draft 4 of the MPC was sent out in 1955 to the states so that the states could revise their sex laws. The full MPC was sent to the states in 1962 for consideration by the states.[40] Numerous states have adopted the code in part or its entirety. Importantly, the MPC includes no penalties for fornication, adultery, or sodomy. States looking to update their criminal code in the 1970s often followed the recommendations of the MPC and reduced or eliminated penalties for these and other similar crimes. Hence, it can be seen, that when considering sexual freedom, elite preferences have played a large role in states changing their laws.

By 1980, Michigan was the least sexually free state in the U.S. This is the result of Michigan having failed to perform a comprehensive overhaul of the criminal code since the 1930s. Most states performed comprehensive updates in the late 1960s, the 1970s, or the early 1980s. In Michigan the penalties for adultery and fornication are felonies and they have not been updated since the 1930s. Although enforcement is not unheard of, these statutes are rarely enforced, which has allowed them to remain on the books without raising public interest or a desire for legal change. It is important to note that even Michigan's seemingly outdated adultery law garnered enough support to prevent from passing a 2009 bill that would have had it repealed.[41]

Figure 4-3 shows, via map chart, the increase in sexual freedom (median voter preference) from 1960 to 2010. One can also see that sexual freedom is generally higher on the East and West coast. Further, most of the change occurs in the 1970's with few changes from 1980 to 2010.

Figure 4-4 shows the average sexual freedom value for each state over the past 51 years. Hawaii shows the most sexual freedom, with Michigan the least sexual freedom. This result is like

---

40. Robinson and Dubber, *The American Model Penal Code: A Brief Overview*, 326–29.

41. 2009 Senate Bill 221 ended up being referred to the Senate Judiciary Committee.

the results using the Innovation Score method. Innovation Scores ranks the "state receptivity for the different laws by comparing a state adoption of law with the first and last state to adopt the innovation."[42] Hawaii, Ohio, Alaska, New Jersey, and Connecticut receive the top 5 innovative states in terms of sexual freedom, whereas the least innovative are Utah, Massachusetts, Wisconsin, Michigan, and Mississippi.[43] Both methods mentioned show similar results.

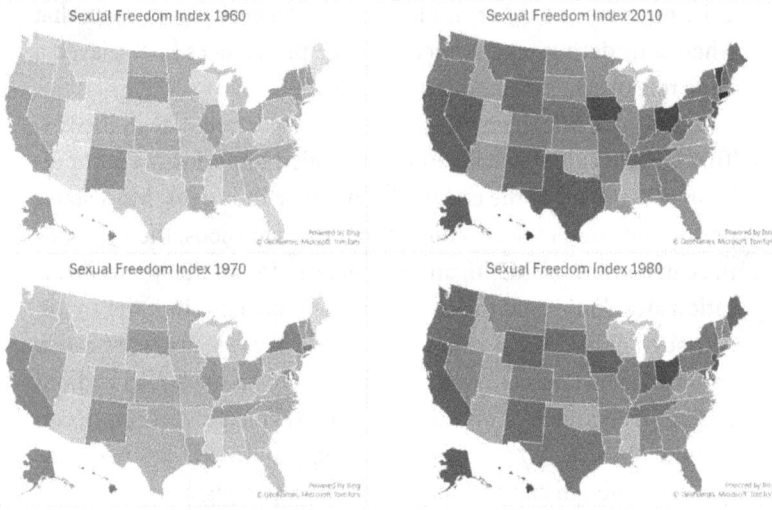

Figure 4-3: Median voter preferred Sexual Freedom Index values from 1960 to 2010 going counter-clockwise from the top left. Darker shades indicate higher Sexual Freedom Index scores.

42. Bose, *Policy Innovativeness and Sexual Freedom*, 6.
43. Bose, *Policy Innovativeness and Sexual Freedom*, 8.

ASSESSING SEXUAL FREEDOM ACROSS THE 50 STATES

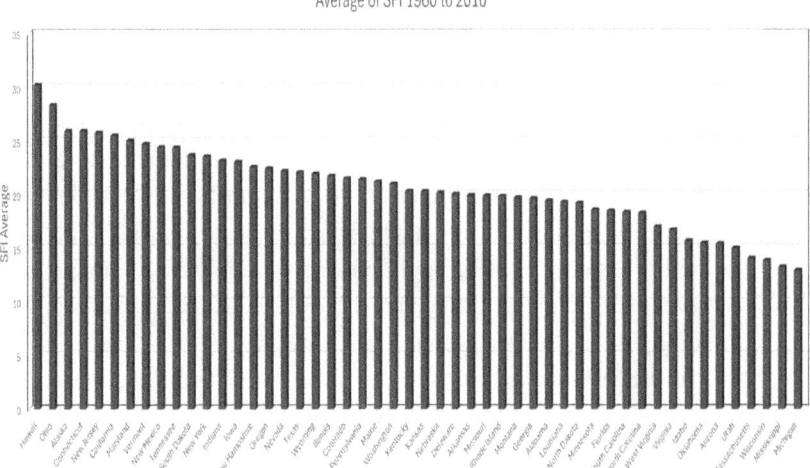

Figure 4-4: Average state-level sexual freedom over 51 years. Hawaii on average has been the freest while Michigan is the least free.

DISCUSSION OF TRENDS BY INDIVIDUAL VARIABLES IN THE SFI

To observe the changes in each variable over time, we will consider the aggregation of all the state values for each variable. We will look at the variables in the two sub-indexes as listed in Table 4-1. When looking at the Marriage Protection Freedom sub-index variables (see Figure 4-5), there is a clear upward shift in freedom relating to adultery, cohabitation, divorce, and miscegenation occurring largely during the 1970s. However, adultery was and continues to be more harshly punished among these four variables. The remaining four variables undergo much less change. Close-blood or familial marriage is essentially unchanging. The legality of close-blood marriage undergoes a few small upward shifts. The legality of homosexual marriage and the recognition of homosexual marriages in other states are, of course, closely related. Both undergo a positive shift beginning around 2000. Polygamy is the only variable in this group that undergoes a negative shift. The legality of polygamous relationships was very low in 1960 but dropped approximately fifteen points throughout the 1960s and 1970s. This is likely the result of codification following or lagging social norms. The states that introduced stricter penalties for polygamy, Alaska, Hawaii, Indiana, Kansas, Minnesota, New Hampshire, North Dakota, and Pennsylvania were likely states that had not needed a statute because the existing social norms were powerful enough to prevent such undesirable behavior. However, Montana and Nebraska slightly loosed polygamy restrictions.

In the second group of variables, the Sex Crimes sub-index, there is a clear upward shift in freedom relating to bestiality, abortion, sodomy, and fornication occurring largely during the 1970s (see Figure 4–6). Abortion and Sodomy undergo dramatic upward shifts. Both begin at near zero aggregate SFI values in 1960 and end at an aggregate value beyond ninety. Bestiality follows these laws with a dramatic shift to increased freedom, but then changes direction and returns to a lower freedom level. This is because many laws penalizing sodomy contained clauses addressing bestiality as well. Many of these sodomy laws were removed during the 1970s, incidentally legalizing bestiality. The social norms regarding bestiality had not likely changed, and over time laws were re-instated to penalize bestiality. This misalignment was corrected as penalties increased to match the prevailing social norms. Age of consent laws, prostitution, and pimp laws show only slight changes during the period studied.

CONCLUSION

Quantifying sexual freedom enables the testing of various hypotheses, including those related to Unwin's theories. The SFI tracks changes in laws related to sexual regulations and the influence of Kinsey's fraudulent research. Over 51 years, the SFI saw a dramatic increase, especially during the 1970s with the introduction of the model penal code. According to Unwin, if the SFI accurately reflects social norms, this increase could lead to total economic collapse within three generations. However, if these changes were primarily driven by elite preferences of the Kinsey Institute, the Rockefeller Foundation, and the American Law Institute (ALI), there may still be hope for the U.S.

In the upcoming chapter, we will explore the different paths to prosperity that economic historians, political economists, and other scholars have proposed. This will set the stage for examining how sexual freedom in society might impede the journey to prosperity in the following chapter.

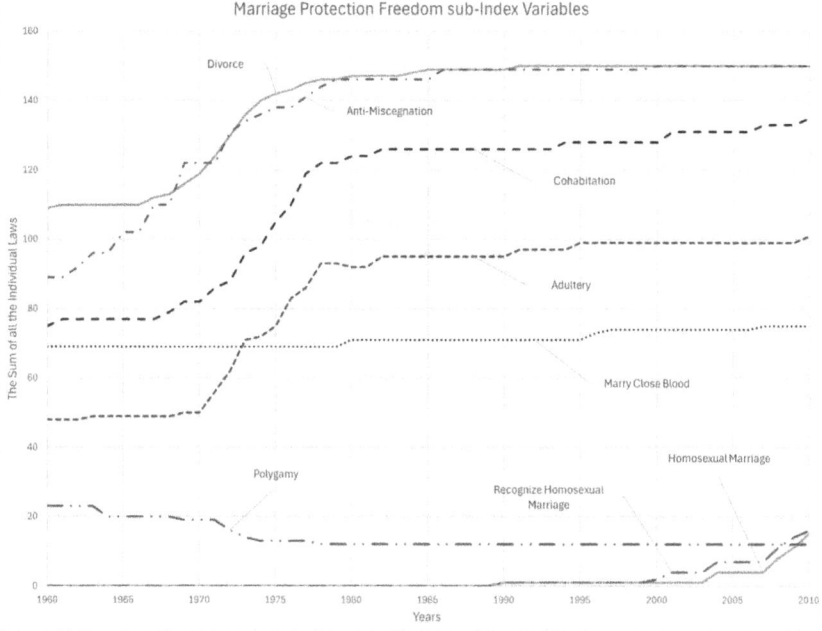

Figure 4-5: Marriage protection variables showing by their increase a decrease in the protection of sanctified marriage. Two of the variables show only minor changes.

SEXUAL FREEDOM AND ITS IMPACT ON ECONOMIC GROWTH AND PROSPERITY

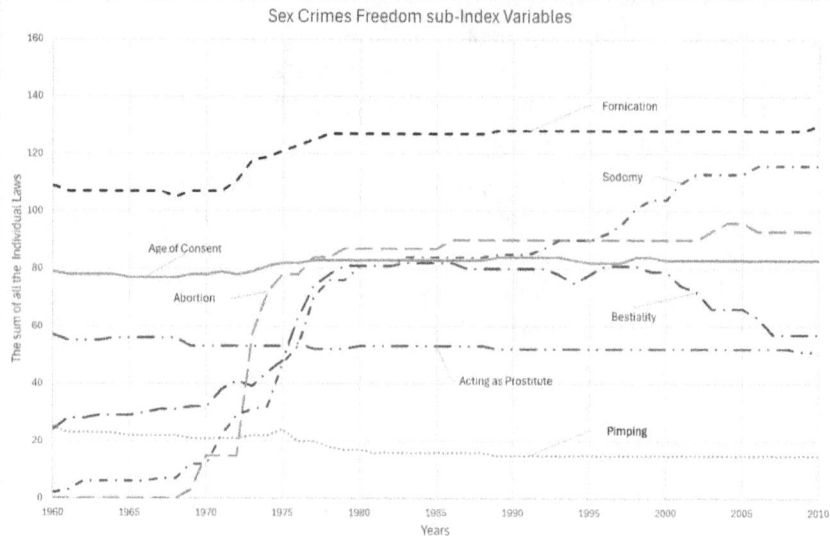

Figure 4-6: Four of the sex crime variables show a dramatic increase over the past 51 years. Rising tolerance for bestiality is reversed. Two of the variables show minor changes.

5

The Paths to Prosperity

Contemporary Theories on Global Wealth Accumulation

So now, return and obey the Lord your God and observe all his commands that I'm giving you today, and the Lord your God will prosper you abundantly in all that you do, along with your children, your livestock, and the produce of your fields, because the Lord your God will again be delighted with you for good, just as he was delighted with your ancestors, if you obey him and keep his commands and statutes that are written in this Book of the Law, and if you return to him with all your heart and soul.

DEUTERONOMY 30:8–10 (ISV)

TO COMPREHEND HOW A thriving and expansive civilization can be achieved, we must first explore the current understanding of the paths to economic growth and prosperity. In this chapter, I will examine various theories on the path to prosperity and lay the groundwork for understanding Unwin's thesis on the connection between sexual freedom and economic growth resulting in prosperity.

The question of how the world became affluent is complex, with no single theory offered by economists and social scientists that is able to explain it fully. The wealth of the world, most of which has accumulated in the last two centuries, is a result of a multitude of factors interacting with each other. These factors, though not exhaustive, include geography, culture/religion, demography, institutions, colonialism, and sexual restraint. This chapter discusses all these factors. Each of these factors plays a role, with some being more prominent than others, and their interplay is crucial to understanding the economic growth that occurred. Understanding economic growth has real-world implications, particularly for those still living in poverty.

The Industrial Revolution, which began in England, is a significant event in this narrative. The reasons why it started when and where it did are multifaceted. Similarly, the reasons why some countries were able to catch up economically, while others lagged, are also complex and varied.

Sustained economic growth is a key factor in this accumulation of wealth. There have been periods of growth throughout history, such as the Commercial Revolution in Europe between 1000 and 1300, the Islamic Golden Age in the Middle East between the 7th and 10th centuries, and the times of Song China, Rome, and other civilizations. However, these periods of growth were not sustained and were often subject to reversals. Many scholars have tried to understand this phenomenon, often emphasizing one factor of growth whether it is geography, institutions, and so on.

However, causal interactions among these factors are important, such as those between culture and institutions or a country's colonial past. Nearly all studies in development focus on Britain, the first country to achieve sustained economic growth in modern times. While the Industrial Revolution started earlier in the 18th century, modern sustained economic growth occurred in the 19th century.

The preconditions that made modern sustained economic growth possible and why it didn't happen elsewhere need to be studied. Before England, the Netherlands was economically advanced; before that, it was Northern Flanders (modern Belgium) and Northern Italy.¹ Additionally, the ideas of prosperity spread to countries like the US and China. Understanding the factors that prospered these economies can provide valuable insights into the path to prosperity.

Figure 5-1 shows history's hockey stick indicating modern sustained economic growth. The sustained economic development started in the United Kingdom and has spread to other countries. Many countries have caught up with the United Kingdom like Japan and France. Countries like the United States have leaped ahead. Furthermore, recently, countries like China and India have also started experiencing sustained economic growth.

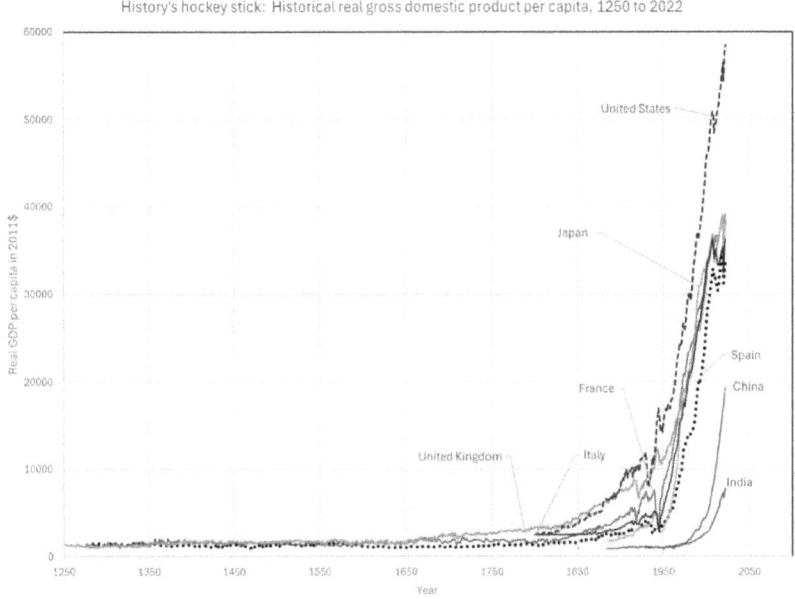

Figure 5-1: History's hockey stick showing sustained economic growth starting with the United Kingdom.²

1. Stark, *The Victory of Reason: How Christianity Led to Freedom, Capitalism, and Western Success*, chapters 3-5.

2. Bolt and van Zanden, *Maddison-Style Estimates of the Evolution of the World Economy: A New 2023 Update*, 1-41.

HOW INSTITUTIONS AFFECT ECONOMIC PROSPERITY

Several economists believe that good institutions are important for economic growth and prosperity. Institutions encompassing political, legal, economic, and religious entities play a pivotal role in shaping economic incentives. They have the potential to explain the reversal of fortunes. Spearheaded by Douglas North, modern institutional literature integrates economic analysis with the study of institutions.

North, a prominent economic historian, defines institutions as "humanly devised constraints that structure political, economic, and social interactions."[3] They consist of both informal constraints and formal rules. Informal constraints include things like taboos, codes of conduct, traditions, and sanctions, whereas formal rules are things like constitutions and laws.

These institutions, according to North, are necessary to "create order and reduce uncertainty in exchange."[4] In other words, they are the "rules of the game" that govern how societies operate and evolve. They play a crucial role in determining the economic performance of different countries.

North's 1981 "Structure and Change in Economic History" posits that there is no process analogous to the competitive market to select the most efficient institutions. Markets weed out inefficient firms, but inefficient institutions can persist for extended periods. Essentially, institutions don't necessarily evolve or get selected based on their efficiency.[5] This insight highlights that incentives in the political sphere differ from those in the marketplace as such institutions can be the root cause of enduring poverty and are also a leading reason why some countries are affluent.

A key aspect of institutions is the extent to which they promote economic freedom. Greater economic freedom means more liberty for individuals and firms have to allocate their resources

---

3. North, *Institutions*, 97.
4. North, *Institutions*, 97.
5. North, *Structure and Change in Economic History*, 7.

as they deem fit. Economic freedom is closely associated with the rule of law.

Institutions that facilitate the rule of law, such as those that constrain the executive branch's power and secure property rights, are key components of economic freedom. Property rights ensure that individuals reap the returns on their investments. The rule of law guarantees that the government will enforce contracts and protect property rights. This enforcement of contracts and protection of property rights facilitates more economic transactions because it ensures a stable and predictable environment for economic activities.

Legal systems play a crucial role. Small-scale societies rely on informal and decentralized legal systems, while large-scale societies have complex legal systems. In Western Europe, checks on the state guarantee individuals a private sphere of non-interference. An article by La Porta, de Silanes, Shleifer, and Vishny, further suggests that English common law offers better protection of property rights compared to civil law countries (French, German, and Scandinavian legal systems). The protection of property is systematically stronger for common law countries.[6]

Institutions however are dependent on factors such as culture, geography, and colonial legacy. These factors interplay in complex ways to shape the trajectory of society's economic growth and development.

HOW GEOGRAPHY AFFECTS ECONOMIC PROSPERITY

Geography encompasses elements such as climate, soil type, mountainous terrain, and access to coasts and rivers. It plays a significant role in the spread of trade and technology. The proximity to the equator also has implications for a region's development. Jared Diamond, in his book "Guns, Germs, and Steel," delves into these geographical aspects of economic development, including

---

6. La Porta, et al., *Law and Finance*, 1113.

the influence of the continental axis. Specifically, Diamond argued that Eurasia, with its dominant east-west axis, had a unique advantage over other regions such as the Americas and Africa, which have a predominant north-south axis.

The east-west axis of Eurasia facilitated the spread of agriculture, technology, and other innovations due to relatively uniform climates and day lengths over vast distances. This contrasts with the Americas and Africa, where the north-south axis and varying climates and ecological zones posed significant barriers to the spread of crops and domesticated animals.[7]

Diamond's hypothesis suggests that these geographical and ecological factors played a crucial role in shaping the disparate rates of economic development and resulted in the dominance of Eurasian civilizations.

Geography also significantly affects disease patterns. The "Malaria Belt" in Africa is a prime example, where the burden of constant disease has led to underdevelopment and underinvestment in human capital.[8]

Geography presents an attractive argument as it is exogenous, i.e., not influenced by other variables of interest, and remains constant. However, geography's influence on culture and institutions adds another layer of complexity.

One of the challenges with geography-based explanations is their constancy. The geography thesis struggles to explain the reversals of fortune observed in history. For example, why was the Middle East or China more developed than Western Europe in 1000 AD, but by 1800 AD, Western Europe had surged ahead?

Infrastructure, such as canals and roads, can mitigate geographical disadvantages. However, the development of such infrastructure varies across states, suggesting that institutions may play a crucial role. Therefore, while geography is a significant factor, it is part of a complex interplay of elements that contribute to economic growth and development.

---

7. Diamond, *Guns Germs and Steel: The Fates of Human Societies*, 176–91.

8. McCord and Sachs, *Physical Geography and the History of Economic Development*, 21.

HOW COLONIZATION AFFECTS ECONOMIC PROSPERITY

Between the 15th and 20th centuries, a small group of European countries embarked on a global colonization mission. This period saw the extraction and exploitation of natural resources from various parts of the world and is often cited as a reason for Europe's accumulation of wealth and the slower economic progress of the rest of the world. However, it's important to note that colonization and poverty are not necessarily directly linked.

The impact of European colonization varied widely, with some countries experiencing transitory colonization and others long-lasting colonial rule. The effects of colonization on the colonized regions were also diverse. Some colonized countries, such as the United States, Canada, Australia, Hong Kong, and Singapore, prospered, while others remained impoverished, particularly in Sub-Saharan Africa.

The type of institutions established by the colonizers significantly influenced the economic and political development of the formerly colonized world. In many cases, extractive institutions were set up by colonists where mortality was higher for the colonizers. This limited the rights of native populations and restricted investments in public goods to those benefiting the colonizers, such as roads from mines to ports. Post-colonial governments often found these extractive institutions useful, leading to their persistence even after independence. This has resulted in persistent bad governance. However, if colonists settled in an area, like the United States, then the rule of law was established. These areas saw quicker wage growth, greater investment in education, improved health facilities, and better infrastructure.[9]

In conclusion, it is crucial to note that the economic impacts of colonization were not uniform but rather varied significantly across different regions for various reasons.

---

9. Acemoglu, et al., *The Colonial Origins of Comparative Development: An Empirical Investigation*, 1395.

HOW DEMOGRAPHY AFFECTS ECONOMIC PROSPERITY

Family structure significantly influences societal development. Factors such as the age of one's first marriage, child mortality rates, birth and death rates, and life expectancy play crucial roles in shaping a society's trajectory. The question arises: how have these factors been key to economic prosperity?

Over the centuries, the increase in life expectancy has had a profound impact on economic growth. Historically, despite high birth rates, few children survived to adulthood. This was the norm, as noted by Malthus at the end of the 18th century. He believed this to be a permanent condition of the human experience, with people barely eking out a living due to food production increasing at an arithmetic rate ("1, 2, 3, 4, 5, 6, 7, 8, 9"), whereas, the population grew at a geometric rate ("1, 2, 4, 8, 16, 32, 64, 128, 256").[10] However, he failed to account for the significant changes in the human condition that have occurred since then.

The transition from a Malthusian world to a world where modern economic growth is possible is a fascinating study. It was found that demographic changes led to changes in human capital, which then impacted economic growth.

The Black Death is one instance of a major demographic change. It resulted in the death of one-third to one-half of Europe's population, providing a stark example of the effects of massive demographic change on economic conditions. Trade collapsed, real wages fell, and food was left rotting in the fields as crops went unharvested. Political elites across Europe attempted to prevent wages from rising, but economic pressures overcame the machinations of the elites. Marginal lands were abandoned, and landowners shifted from labor-intensive arable farming to more land-intensive pastoral farming. The most significant institutional consequence of the Black Death was the end of serfdom in Western Europe. The demographic shock made it impossible for landlords to maintain serfdom.[11]

---

10. Malthus, *An Essay on the Principle of Population*, Book 1 Chapter 1.
11. Koyama and Rubin, *How the World Became Rich: The Historical Origins*

Another demographic transition began in the 19th century and resulted in lower birth and death rates. Smaller family sizes helped societies escape the Malthusian trap. Late marriages also contributed to having fewer children, significantly reducing fertility. The so-called European Marriage Pattern, as described by Hajnal in 1965, helped keep per capita incomes higher than they would have otherwise been. Hajnal thinks the marriage pattern could be linked to the protestant ethic. This pattern, characterized by late marriages, played a crucial role in shaping economic outcomes as resources accumulated before marriage are diverted to tools and capital beyond what is required for minimum subsistence for the future family.[12]

HOW CULTURE AFFECTS ECONOMIC PROSPERITY: INTRODUCTION

Culture encompasses various factors such as racial norms, ethical norms, religious values, the value placed on education, trust in outsiders, family structures, incest taboos, and so on. It is a rapidly expanding field of study. Defined by cultural anthropologists, culture is a set of learned rules of behavior. These rules serve as shortcuts to help us make sense of a complex world, given our limited cognitive capacity. They encompass learned norms and beliefs. Many cultural norms persist today and arose in the distant past. In today's changing world they play an important role in affecting economic growth. Culture also interacts with other determinants of economic growth such as institutions and demography.

The question remains how might culture aid or impede development? Culture does affect economic outcomes. Guiso et al., focuses on prior beliefs, values, or preferences, to show the causal effect from culture to economic outcomes.[13] Moreover, cultural development evolves at a slower pace than technological

---

of Economic Growth, 92–96.

   12. Hajnal, *European Marriage Patterns in Perspective*, 101, 32.

   13. Guiso, et al., *Does Culture Affect Economic Outcomes?*, 24.

and economic change. Cultural beliefs can be maladapted to their economic environment, which could be a reason why some parts of the world fell behind. For instance, some cultural values are against work and profit. The ancient Romans considered work, especially manual labor, to be the lowest of pursuits and that physical work was to be done by slaves. The goal of the free man then was to attain an "honorable retirement into rural peace as a country gentleman" by having others do the work. Wealth was desirable so one could live in a villa and relax.[14] In contrast, some cultures, especially more recently in history, value ingenuity, technological development, and hands-on work.[15]

Peter T. Bauer was an early development economist who critiqued mainstream development experts who advocated for central planning, foreign aid, and protectionism. He asserts that there is an undeniable existence of certain deep-rooted attitudes, beliefs, and cultural traditions in many underdeveloped nations that are not conducive to material progress. These elements are intertwined and have been present for a long time, often accompanied by a relative lack of personal abilities that would otherwise promote progress. Hence, he believed that the key to development is the character of its people.

Furthermore, Bauer suggests that these factors, unfavorable to material advancement, have been in place for such a long time that it is highly unlikely that they will be eradicated or even significantly diminished soon. This is particularly true when considering the relatively short timeframe of a few years or even decades. The persistence of these factors could potentially hinder the pace of development in these countries.

> Examples of significant attitudes, beliefs and modes of conduct unfavorable to material progress include lack of interest in material advance, combined with resignation in the face of poverty; lack of initiative, self-reliance and a sense of personal responsibility for the economic fortune

---

14. Tilgher, *Work: What It Has Meant to Men through the Ages (Homo Faber)*, 8.

15 Lipset, *The Work Ethic, Then and Now*, 45.

of oneself and one's family; high leisure preference, together with a lassitude often found in tropical climates; relatively high prestige of passive or contemplative life compared to active life; the prestige of mysticism and of renunciation of the world compared to acquisition and achievement; acceptance of the idea of a preordained, unchanging and unchangeable universe; emphasis on performance of duties and acceptance of obligations, rather than on achievement or results, or assertion or even recognition of personal rights; lack of sustained curiosity, experimentation and interest in change; belief in the efficacy of supernatural and occult forces and of their influence over one's destiny; insistence on the unity of the organic universe, and on the need to live with nature rather than conquer it or harness it to man's needs, an attitude of which reluctance to take animal life is a corollary; belief in perpetual reincarnation, which reduces the significance of effort in the course of the present life; recognized status of beggary, together with a lack of stigma in the acceptance of charity; opposition to women's work outside the household.[16]

Bauer emphasizes that these attitudes "are not surface phenomena," but are "an integral part of the spiritual and emotional life" of hundreds of millions of people.[17] Hence if this is true, then how did the change occur that resulted in sustained economic growth these past 200 or so years in Northwestern Europe? What old cultural attitudes changed to allow for this sustained economic growth?

HOW RELIGION AFFECTS ECONOMIC PROSPERITY

Religion is an important driver of culture. As Max Weber argued, religion plays an important role in economic development. The Calvinist doctrine of predestination encouraged people to work

16. Bauer, *Dissent on Development: Studies and Debates in Development Economics*, 78–79.
17. Bauer, *Dissent on Development: Studies and Debates in Development Economics*, 79.

hard and save (asceticism) and was a divinely approved method within one's God-given calling. The ethic demonstrated that they were among the elect and hence blessed. Hence, predestination is a causal factor in releasing the spirit of capitalism.[18]

> When the limitation of consumption is combined with this release of acquisitive activity, the inevitable practical result is obvious: accumulation of capital through ascetic compulsion to save. The restraints which were imposed upon the consumption of wealth naturally served to increase it by making possible the productive investment of capital ... the greater simplicity of life in the more seriously religious circles, in combination with great wealth, led to an excessive propensity to accumulations.[19]

Many studies show that Protestantism is positively correlated with economic growth. However, is this a causal relationship? Did Protestantism, especially Calvinism, cause economic growth due to a stronger work ethic, or is there another explanation? Is it merely a correlation? Weber's thesis has faced numerous critiques.

If it is not the capitalist work ethic, then what other reasons could explain why Protestant countries grew faster? Factors such as schooling for both boys and girls, political economy, and bureaucratization are more associated with Protestantism than with other religions and are important factors of development. Arruñada further compares Protestants and Catholics and finds Protestantism is better conducive to economic growth not because of the Weberian work ethic, but rather a 'social ethic' that promotes impersonal trade and thus markets. The Reformation lowered the "transaction costs of impersonal trade" as it made values more homogenous among Christians due to its emphasis on education and "universal charity and its greater reliance on 'external' sources for enforcement."[20]

---

18. Weber, *The Protestant Ethic and the Spirit of Capitalism*, 141, 57–59, 62, 72.

19. Weber, *The Protestant Ethic and the Spirit of Capitalism*, 172–73.

20. Arruñada, *Protestants and Catholics: Similar Work Ethic, Different Social Ethic*, 895.

When looking at Islam, how does Islam and the culture it fosters encourage or discourage economic growth? Islamic countries were prosperous between the 7th and 10th centuries, but when looking at Islamic countries today there is a negative correlation between the presence of Islam and economic development. Is there something about Islam that hindered economic development? Are there attributes of Islam that hinder economic growth in more recent times but helped economic growth at other times? Timur Kuran has researched the role Islamic institutions played in developing the Middle East. Kuran writes about how certain Islamic beliefs, especially those tied to inheritance laws, resulted in stagnant institutions that hindered entrepreneurship and firm longevity, resulting in lower economic performance. Inheritance laws, which, upon the death of a successful entrepreneur, divided the firm's assets among heirs, preventing the company from remaining intact across generations.[21]

On the other hand, in West Africa, Islamic institutions fostered long-distance trade as it brought "a common language of trade (Arabic), a monetary system, an accounting system, and a legal code to adjudicate financial contracts and disputes," leading to prosperity in the region compared to previous polytheist societies.[22] Further trust in various agents was closely linked to their adherence to Islamic practices, such as fasting during Ramadan, building mosques, and undertaking the Hajj pilgrimage. This brief survey shows that religion does impact economic growth and prosperity.

HOW CULTURE AFFECTS ECONOMIC PROSPERITY: REVALUATION OF THE BOURGEOISIE

McCloskey and Carden wrote that during the 16th and 17th centuries, Europe transformed from revolts, revolution, reformation,

---

21. Kuran, *Why the Middle East Is Economically Underdeveloped: Historical Mechanisms of Institutional Stagnation*, 74.

22. Ensminger, *Transaction Costs and Islam: Explaining Conversion in Africa*, 7.

and reading to a fifth R, that is revaluation of the bourgeoisie. What was initially considered disreputable, that is, the activities of shopkeepers, merchants, and innovators, was now seen as reputable. This shift in attitude resulted in multiple increases in material well-being. The evidence of change in attitude was seen in writings and the stage. The "great enrichment" which started in the 1500s sped up in the 1700s, and exponentially in the 1800s. During this time, the reading material flowed out of the printing presses, the Protestant Reformation changed church governance, and the 80-year war, where the Dutch gained independence, wiped out the aristocracy, resulting in rule by the burghers and businesspeople, which later the English copied, resulting in their growth as well.[23]

McCloskey basic argument was that a cultural transformation is needed so that an economy could transform to a powerhouse. When wealth creation was no longer seen as contemptible, then it could be created to a grander extent. McCloskey argues that the essence of the bourgeois spirit, that is, a subtle appreciation of labor, the art of tinkering, and the pursuit of betterment through the mechanisms of trade and commerce when it became the mainstream culture, helped with the take off.[24]

Boudreaux, writing about McCloskey's three-volume work on *The Bourgeois Era*, summarizes the era before the cultural change that resulted in the revaluation of the bourgeoisie which caused the economic take off period.

> Unlike warriors who dirtied their hands honorably (namely, with blood), traders dirtied their hands dishonorably (namely, with profit). Unlike the nobility who got their riches honorably (namely, by idly collecting land rents), merchants got their riches dishonorably (namely, by actively trading). Unlike the clergy who won their rewards honorably (namely, by pondering the eternal), the bourgeoisie won their rewards dishonorably.[25]

23. McCloskey and Carden, *Leave Me Alone and I'll Make You Rich: How the Bourgeois Deal Enriched the World*, 94–95,171–75.

24. McCloskey and Carden, *Leave Me Alone and I'll Make You Rich: How the Bourgeois Deal Enriched the World*, 135–42.

25. Boudreaux, Donald J. Boudreaux, "Deirdre Mccloskey and Economists'

Discussing McCloskey's work, Mokyr has properly pointed out that "Culture cannot be understood without institutions, just as institutions cannot be understood without culture."[26] That it is not one or other option. These two factors interact though many economists choose sides on which is more important. Culture and institutions may be self-reinforcing, but to play chicken and egg with them, you need to think of what may happen when they are in discord.

Rose suggests that a low trust society cannot create and sustain highly trust dependent institutions. He further asks the question of why low trust societies, which are poor, do not simply adopt institutions that support high levels of trust. Low-trust societies cannot "simply adopt institutions to produce a high-trust society because the causation runs the other way."[27] A high level of trust in society leads to the creation of trust dependent institutions. In other words, the causal relationship is that culture influences the development of institutions.

HOW CULTURE AFFECTS ECONOMIC PROSPERITY: TIME AND CLOCKS

In his influential paper, "Time, Work-Discipline, and Industrial Capitalism," E.P. Thompson writes about the importance of the development of clocks resulting in industrialism. Three key observations can be made about what he calls task-oriented societies which are typically peasant and non-industrial societies. First, task orientation is more relatable and understandable from a human perspective than time-bound labor. Second, in task-oriented societies, there seems to be a minimal distinction between "work" and "life." The length of the workday can be longer or shorter based on the task at hand, and, for this reason, there is hardly any significant conflict between work and leisurely activities. Lastly, for those who

---

Ideas About Ideas, section 1.

  26 Mokyr, *False Dichotomy*, last paragraph.

  27. Rose, *The Moral Foundations of Economic Behavior*, 208.

are accustomed to time-regulated work, task-oriented labor might seem inefficient and lacking in urgency.

The arrival of clocks was slow and public clocks started to appear in England in the 14th century, and by the end of the 16th century, most communities had them. In the mid-1600s, the introduction of the pendulum advanced the accuracy of household clocks. Other advances in the "escapement and the spiral balance-spring" in the late 1600s improved the accuracy of pocket watches. By the 1800s, there were plenty of watches and clocks in the marketplace.

When people work, they often need to do their tasks at the same time. This is called synchronization. When the work is done in small workshops or at home and does not involve many different steps, there is not much need for synchronization. People can focus on one task at a time.

In the past, workers had to do a lot of extra jobs like fetching and carrying materials. Bad weather could cause problems. For example, when finished cloth had to be stretched out to dry, and this couldn't be done in the rain. For this reason, work patterns alternated between periods of intense labor and idleness. The workweek also showed irregularity in terms of work done. Some irregular work dynamics were due to heavy drinking that occurred on weekends. A rhyme from 1639 illustrates this:

> You know that Munday is Sundayes brother;
> Tuesday is such another;
> Wednesday you must go to Church and pray;
> Thursday is half-holiday;
> On Friday it is too late to begin to spin;
> The Saturday is half-holiday agen[28]

Moreover, the irregular work week also spills over to the irregular work year due to things like holidays, fairs, saints' days, customary wakes and feasts, and so on. These issues have persisted into the 1900s and still occur in many parts of the world.

---

28. Thompson, *Time, Work-Discipline, and Industrial Capitalism*, 72.

So how did the transition to industrial capitalism occur under these circumstances? How did the transition to synchronized labor and stricter time routines arise for industrial capitalism to take off? There is no single way for the transition to take place. "The stress of the transition falls upon the whole culture: resistance to change and assent to change arise from the whole culture. And this culture includes the systems of power, property-relations, religious institutions, etc., inattention to which merely flattens phenomena and trivializes analysis."[29]

To get to industrial capitalism, a need for time thrift, time discipline, and time sense must predominate all classes of people. Time discipline is the knowledge of time combined with obedience resulting in adhering to activities, which increases productivity and coordination. Time thrift means clock-watching and realizing every moment is precious or the notion "time is money." Time sense is an awareness and perception of time passing.[30] These things came together, at least in England, in the late 1700s. According to Thompson, the Puritan ethic was key to it all coming together. The promotion of industry and the moral condemnation of laziness were emphasized strongly by the Puritans who adopted the new discipline on themselves and encouraged the working class also. The interior "moral time-piece" had to be in order before the pocket watch made a difference. Thompson quoting Baxter, says that the theme of redeeming the time is important: 'use every minute of it as a most precious thing, and spend it wholly in the way of duty.'[31]

The use of public clocks helped people better plan their activities due to easier coordination and organization and reduced transaction time.

In a working paper, Lars Boerner and Battista Severgnini found that the early adopters of the mechanical clock technology had a big impact on economic growth and saw an increase

---

29. Thompson, *Time, Work-Discipline, and Industrial Capitalism*, 80.

30. Landes, *Revolution in Time: Clocks and the Making of the Modern World*, 2, 7, 91.

31. Thompson, *Time, Work-Discipline, and Industrial Capitalism*, 87.

in population growth. Further, they found that "general purpose technologies" can greatly influence economic growth though the effects of such groundbreaking innovations are not immediate. Additionally, they find that clocks impact long-term orientation by facilitating coordination and organization.[32] For the technology to have a meaningful impact, it must be culturally and socially accepted across various economic sectors. They found: "technological change [when] embedded in institutional and cultural change results in long-run economic growth."[33] Hence, their idea ties in with Thompson's idea that both supply and demand for technology must come together fostering a long-term orientation leading to prosperity.

WHY EUROPE GREW FIRST?

The question of why Europe, specifically Northwestern Europe, became the first region to experience wealth accumulation can be traced back to various preconditions that emerged between 1450 and 1700. These preconditions were political, cultural, geographical, colonial, and demographic in nature.

By 1700, no global economy exhibited signs of sustained growth. Sustained growth was a phenomenon characterized by a shift from agriculture to industry and services, increased urbanization, demographic changes leading to lower birth and death rates, and a crucial surge in innovation rates. These elements coalesced in Northwestern Europe during the 18th and 19th centuries, triggering sustained growth (see Figure 5–1).

The focus from the Netherlands that started the initial economic growth is then followed and overtaken by Britain, where the onset of modern economic growth is observed. The commencement of industrialization and a surge in GDP marked this period. Technological progress was pivotal, with the rate of innovation skyrocketing and continuing to thrive even today. This economic

---

32. Boerner and Severgnini, *Time for Growth*, 16.
33. Boerner and Severgnini, *Time for Growth*, 45.

advancement has shown no signs of waning due to the strength of ongoing innovation.[34]

CONCLUSION

In this chapter, we learned about various paths to prosperity and why some societies experienced prosperity while others did not. The emergence of the modern economy was influenced by geography, institutions, culture, demography, and colonization. These explanations are typically noncontroversial in academia. However, a key variable that needs a more in-depth analysis is the time variable, and specifically the extension of time horizons that occurred because of the Reformation. The next chapter delves into the time variable, setting the stage for understanding Unwin's thesis. According to Unwin's thesis, sexual freedom and economic freedom are incompatible, and societies with high levels of sexual freedom cannot sustain long-term economic prosperity.

---

34. Koyama and Rubin, *How the World Became Rich: The Historical Origins of Economic Growth*, 147–48.

6

Time Preferences and its link to Economic Freedom and Sexual Freedom

Vincit qui se vincit: Latin: He conquers who conquers himself.

"A good man leaves an inheritance to his children's children."
PROVERBS 13:22A (KJV)

IN THIS CHAPTER, I will explain the concept of time preferences and how it ties with sexual freedom and economic freedom and provide the causal story for Unwin's thesis.

In Aesop's fable of the grasshopper and ant, a grasshopper spent the warm months in song, while an industrious ant toiled to gather winter provisions. As winter fell, the starving grasshopper pleaded with the ant for sustenance. When questioned about its summer activities, the grasshopper confessed to singing away the time. The ant, unimpressed by its frivolity, chided the grasshopper for its lack of foresight and suggested it sing and dance away the winter, mirroring its summer idleness. This fable serves as a reminder of the importance of planning for the future and having longer time horizons; this is important for building civilizations.

TIME PREFERENCE: A SURVEY

Time preference is the degree to which the future is considered. It can also be seen as the degree to which people favor the 'sooner' or current goods versus the 'later' or future goods. Time horizons, a related concept, is the relevant length of time over which an investment is made, or a decision is considered. A long-time horizon means that a person is concerned about events in the distant future. A similar concept is patience. Being patient signifies one's willingness to forego present consumption in exchange for (greater) future consumption—thus placing significant importance on future occurrences. Economists have further developed the idea of the "discount rate" to measure a person's present orientation or degree of impatience.[1]

Time preferences and time horizons are different in "primitive" hunter-gatherer societies when compared to modern capitalistic societies. The concepts of time preference and time horizon are important determinants of economic growth and societal change. Time preference is related to the ideas of delayed gratification or delayed pleasure which is different from person to person. Children delaying gratification on average do better later in life.[2]

What causes time preference to vary across countries and throughout different periods in history? What are the economic, social, institutional, and religious elements that shape the time horizons of individuals, as well as economic and political decision-makers? These are significant inquiries that have only recently been studied by economists.

The examination of historical factors that influence time preference is primarily motivated by a central question: Are we capable of understanding the underlying causes that have led to changes in

---

1. Ikeda, *The Economics of Self-Destructive Choices*, 7.
2. Mischel, et al., *Delay of Gratification in Children*, 937.

time preference and the broadening of time horizons? This question is crucial because it helps us evaluate whether the current trajectory of change in time preference is still on the 'right' path.

Over time, economic and political institutions have evolved, and this evolution may have inadvertently created an environment where policymakers and entrepreneurs are pressured to secure short-term 'victories', at the expense of a long-term outlook. This raises a critical question: Is there an inherent conflict between the escalating necessity to plan for the future, effectively extending the time horizon, and the prevalent short-term focus that characterizes modern politics and business?[3]

Most indices in the literature on time horizons and patience show a strong positive relationship with GDP (Gross Domestic Product) per capita. That is, where there is more patience in a society it is tied to higher levels of prosperity. Yet, the cause-and-effect relationship is not clearly defined.

TIME PREFERENCE: MEASUREMENT AND IMPLICATIONS

There are three ways researchers have measured time preferences. Each of these methods has its advantages and drawbacks. The first method is obtained by people stating their preferences in surveys like the World Values Survey (WVS). By examining how people respond to questions related to time preference, such as the desirability of thrift as a trait for children, we can understand how different cultures ideally value time. The difficulty with creating an index of time preferences from the questions asked is that it is not clear which questions to include in the index. Hence, this is a more subjective method.

The second method is to use a more objective approach by looking at economic data, specifically the interest rate, as it ties in the future versus the present. That is, interest rates emerge naturally from the interaction of time preferences. "The saver exchanges

---

3. Smith, *Time and Public Policy*, 102.

present (consumer) goods for future (capital) goods with the expectation that these will help produce a larger supply of present goods in the future."[4] The setback here is that central banks can manipulate interest rates below the "natural rate" of interest (the rate that reflects the time preferences of the market participants) as seen recently when central banks artificially lowered interest rates close to zero percent.

The third method to understanding time preferences originates from the fields of experimental economics and psychology. This method involves conducting controlled experiments to measure individual time preferences. A well-known example of such an experiment is the 'Marshmallow Test'. In this test, individuals, typically children, are presented with a choice: they can either consume a marshmallow immediately or delay their gratification and receive a second marshmallow after some time. This test measures the importance of self-control and the ability to delay gratification and its future implications for personal development and success.[5]

Along with others of its kind, this test provides valuable insights into how individuals value immediate versus delayed rewards. It is a practical demonstration of the concept of time preference in action. The decisions made by the individuals in these tests reflect their personal discount rates— the rate at which they discount future rewards in favor of immediate ones.

Research in this area has also revealed that the real discount rate is not a fixed, unchanging value. Instead, it follows a hyperbolic pattern. This means that the discount rate is exceptionally high for decisions involving immediate and smaller rewards. However, as the duration increases and the sums of money involved become larger, the discount rate decreases significantly.[6] This is known as hyperbolic discounting and results in various and common impulse-control issues, and subsequently, various strategies to address them.

---

4. Hoppe, *Democracy the God That Failed: The Economics and Politics of Monarcy, Democracy, and Natural Order*, 6.

5 Mischel, et al., *Delay of Gratification in Children*, 937.

6. Frederick, et al., *Time Discounting and Time Preference: A Critical Review*, 360–61.

> [H]yperbolic discounting conceives the self-control problem as a conflict between a long-term and a short-term self. Both of these selves reside inside one person: a long-term self (angel) who considers the person's long-term benefits, a short-term self (devil) who considers the person's short-term benefits. The angel makes a wonderful long-term action plan with a low discount rate, but it is the devil that carries out the plan each day. With a higher degree of impatience, the devil breaks the future-oriented long-term plan that the angel made, and thereby the individual falls into the intemperance and self-indulgence of pursuing his or her own short-term benefits.[7]

Because of self-control problems due to hyperbolic discounting, individuals have come up with strategies to deal with the self-destructive choices they make. For instance, people often limit the amount of snacks and treats they have at home to avoid overeating. Similarly, individuals enroll in payroll-deduction savings plans to resist the temptation to spend cash in their checking accounts. Many people avoid starting a Netflix series the night before an important meeting, knowing they might struggle to stop halfway. Reformed smokers often prefer the company of nonsmokers when they first attempt to quit and are more likely to support laws that restrict smoking in public places.[8]

It's also worth noting that societies worldwide have implemented various policies to alleviate the effects of impulse-control issues. These include prohibiting gambling, addictive drugs, and prostitution, and imposing sanctions against adultery. Programs designed to encourage savings can also be seen as a response to impulse-control problems that hinder the execution of rational savings plans. We also see this in the Biblical story of Joseph, who implements a tax of one-fifth of the crops produced in Egypt during the seven years of plenty which are then stored in preparation for the seven years of famine.[9]

---

7. Ikeda, *The Economics of Self-Destructive Choices*, 15.

8. Ikeda, *The Economics of Self-Destructive Choices*, 18, 19.

9. The Genesis account suggests that within two years, the Egyptians exhausted their grain reserves from the seven years of plenty and became reliant

Frederick et al. also deduced however, that there have been "no longitudinal studies have been conducted to permit any conclusions about the temporal stability of time preference" (meaning we lack knowledge about historical changes over time), and the "correlations between various measures of time preference or between measures of time preference and plausible real-world expressions of it are modest, at best" (the experimental studies discount rates do not correlate in any way to with 'real world' discount rates in capital markets).[10]

A new method, pioneered by Falk and his team, merges the survey methodology with the expertise garnered from experimental research (first and third methods). The survey questions are linked to various factors such as risk aversion, discounting, trust, altruism, and both positive and negative reciprocity. These variables have been rigorously tested and validated in field experiments, lending credibility to the method.[11]

While this measure has shown promise, it falls short of helping us comprehend historical changes. That is, how does time preference change over the years and decades in a country? This is a crucial aspect that needs to be addressed to gain a comprehensive understanding of time preferences and time horizons.

The study of time preference and time horizons is of paramount importance due to the positive correlation they share with numerous and significant metrics. These include life expectancy, income and wealth, and economic growth, among others. This correlation was highlighted in the studies conducted by Sunde et al.[12] In essence, the exploration of time preferences and time horizons has real-world implications.

Historical trends seem to suggest a shift from a foraging lifestyle to one based on agriculture. This transition inherently

---

on Joseph's stored grain.

10. Frederick, et al., *Time Discounting and Time Preference: A Critical Review*, 391.

11. Falk, et al., *The Preference Survey Module: A Validated Instrument for Measuring Risk, Time, and Social Preferences*, 1935.

12. Sunde, et al., *Patience and Comparative Development*, 2812–24.

required a longer time horizon. Agriculture necessitated the postponement of immediate consumption in exchange for increased output and consumption at a later stage. This is not to say that hunter-gatherers did not consider the future, but the nature of their planning was fundamentally different.

The concept of the afterlife, which is almost universally present in various religions, also contributed to the development of future-oriented thinking. This notion influenced attitudes towards saving, investing, and patience, as it introduced the idea of rewards or consequences in an afterlife. However, the notion of whether the future is cyclical and repetitive (Buddhism, Hinduism) or linear and progressive (Christianity, Judaism) does make a difference in future orientation.[13] The linear view of time was one important factor in the "widespread cultivation of invention."[14]

> Other societies thought of time as cyclical, returning to earlier stages and starting over again. Linear time is progressive or regressive, moving on to better things or declining from some earlier, happier state. For Europeans in our period, the progressive view prevailed.[15]

One method by which Western society fostered behavior aligned with a longer time horizon was through the establishment of corporations. These corporations outlasted their members, becoming, in a sense, everlasting. The Church is a prime example, but the corporate model also flourished in Medieval Europe with the rise of communes, monastic orders (and monasteries), brotherhoods, and guilds. The creation of such organizations was facilitated by aligning their members' short-term interests with the institution's long-term goals.[16,17] For instance, clergy members

---

13. Rushdoony, *Systematic Theology in Two Volumes*, 1109.

14. Gruden and Asmus, *The Poverty of Nations: A Sustainable Solution*, 342.

15. Landes, *The Wealth and Poverty of Nations: Why Some Are So Rich and Some So Poor*, 59.

16. Kuran, *The Scale of Entrepreneurship in Middle Eastern History: Inhibitive Roles of Islamic Institutions*, 68.

17. Richardson, *Craft Guilds and Christianity in Late-Medieval England: A Rational-Choice Analysis*, 139–41.

were motivated to enhance the Church's resources and stature, as this simultaneously elevated their status and income. The development of capitalism requires long-term horizons and investments in fixed capital or long-term assets.

EXPLAINING UNWIN'S THESIS: TIME PREFERENCES AND ITS LINK TO ECONOMIC FREEDOM AND SEXUAL FREEDOM

Time preferences play a role in human action. Individuals with high time preferences live for the moment, are impatient, impulsive with less self-control.[18] They discount the future more and hence fear the future less. This could manifest in various ways, such as making impromptu decisions or prioritizing short-term pleasures over long-term benefits and committing crime. Those with low time preferences delay gratification, plan for the future, and are seen as patient and strategic.[19] They discount the future less. These individuals are likely to exhibit behaviors such as saving for retirement, investing in their education, or maintaining a healthy lifestyle. Time preferences can vary with individuals, groups, and societies. If an individual's time preference is zero, that means consumption is zero and all income is saved and invested.

The concept of time preference is closely related to self-control, which is defined as *"the ability to manage or regulate impulses and desires . . . rather than being managed or regulated by them"* (italics in original).[20] Self-control is a crucial aspect of human behavior and plays a significant role in achieving personal and professional success.

A lack of self-control manifests in various ways. It can lead to "elevated emotional instability, tendency to fly off the handle, low tolerance for frustration, lack of persistence, short attention span, high distractibility, frequent shifting from activity to activity, being

18. Peters and Büchel, *The Neural Mechanisms of Inter-Temporal Decision-Making: Understanding Variability*, 227.

19. Mulligan, *Religion as Adaptation: The Role of Time Preference* 70.

20. Belsky, et al., *The Origins of You: How Childhood Shapes Later Life*, 53.

restless, being overactive, acting before thinking, having problems waiting for something good, and having difficulty taking turns."[21] These behaviors have significant implications for an individual's personal and professional life, affecting their relationships, career progression, and well-being. This also affects society.

Banfield further defines the class position of individuals in terms of time horizons and applies it to various factors including sexual behavior. He states:

> In the analysis to come, the individual's orientation toward the future will be regarded as a function of two factors: (1) ability to imagine a future, and (2) ability to discipline oneself to sacrifice present for future satisfaction. The more distant the future the individual can imagine and can discipline himself to make sacrifices for, the "higher" his class. The criterion, it should be noted, is ability, not performance... It must again be strongly emphasized that this use of the term *class* is different from the ordinary one. As the term is used here, a person who is poor, unschooled, and of low status may be upper-class; indeed he is upper class if he is psychologically capable of providing for a distant future. By the same token, one who is rich and a member of "the 400" may be lower class; he is lower-class if he is incapable of conceptualizing the future or of controlling his impulses and is therefore obliged to live from moment to moment.[22] (italics in original).

Further, Banfield states:

> At the present-oriented end of the scale, the lower-class individual lives from moment to moment. If he has any awareness of a future, it is of something fixed, fated, beyond his control: things happen *to* him, he does not *make* them happen. Impulse governs his behavior, either because *he* cannot discipline himself to sacrifice a present for a future satisfaction or because he has no sense of

---

21. Belsky, et al., *The Origins of You: How Childhood Shapes Later Life*, 53.
22. Banfield, *The Unheavenly City: The Nature and Future of Our Urban Crisis*, 47–48.

the future. He is therefore radically improvident: whatever he cannot use immediately he considers valueless.[23] (italics in original).

In the sexual marketplace, the notion of time preference and time horizon also applies. Individuals with high time preferences live for the moment. They prioritize immediate satisfaction, often driven by impulsive desires, where bodily needs take precedence, leading to a lifestyle of sexual libertinism.[24] On the other hand, individuals with low time preferences are those who are more likely to control their impulses, including sexual ones by waiting for marriage, to secure a stable future.

Banfield writes that the "lower classes" (those with high time preferences) have no sense of the future. A lower-class individual considers his "bodily needs (especially for sex) . . . take precedence over everything else— certainly over any work routine . . . In his relations with others he is suspicious and hostile, aggressive yet dependent. He is unable to maintain a stable relationship with a mate; commonly he does not marry. He feels no attachment to community, neighbors, or friends (he has companions, not friends), resents all authority."[25] Further, future-oriented (lower time preference) cultures teach "the individual that he would be cheating himself if he allowed gratification of his impulses (for example, for sex or violence) to interfere with his provision for the future."[26]

23. Banfield, *The Unheavenly City: The Nature and Future of Our Urban Crisis*, 53.

24. Someone who commits adultery prioritizes their immediate happiness without considering the long-term consequences for their family and community. Individuals in homosexual relationships, being biologically unable to have children, will lack a cross-generational perspective. Those who engage in sex before marriage demonstrate a lack of restraint, opting not to wait for the more secure bond of marriage. Additionally, the castration of transgender youth, which results in sterility, will lead to higher time preferences as time horizons are shorter.

25. Banfield, *The Unheavenly City: The Nature and Future of Our Urban Crisis*, 53.

26. Banfield, *The Unheavenly City: The Nature and Future of Our Urban Crisis*, 49.

In terms of economic freedom, low time preference individuals are more likely to accumulate capital, intending to pass wealth to the next generation. This is often facilitated by a society that has a stable monetary and legal system that encourages savings and protects property rights. Conversely, high time preference individuals may find their savings discouraged due to say taxes on interest. Further, in an environment where property rights are not protected, and high taxes are imposed, these individuals will struggle to secure their economic future.

Even in the animal kingdom, we see the notion of time preferences play out. Monkeys in zoos, a welfare society, are absorbed with sex and present orientation. Whereas in the wild, monkeys are preoccupied with finding food, protecting their young, marking territory, and defending against enemies and in a sense oriented towards the future. In the zoo, all their needs are met, and, in a sense, they are prisoners. "All have traded the hard rules of nature for the more tolerant mastery [slavery] of man."[27]

In Figure 6–1, a society where individuals predominantly have high time preferences (solid line) tends to favor sexual freedom. This is because the median voter position (X'_{med}) is towards the high time preference side, leading politicians to align their platforms with the median voter to attract the broadest possible support. Conversely, in a society where low time preference individuals predominate (dashed curve), society prioritizes economic freedom. Here, the median voter position (X''_{med}) is located towards the low time preference side. This latter scenario leads to economic growth.

---

27. Ardrey, *African Genesis: A Personal Investigation in the Animal Origins and Nature of Man*, 100 and 20.

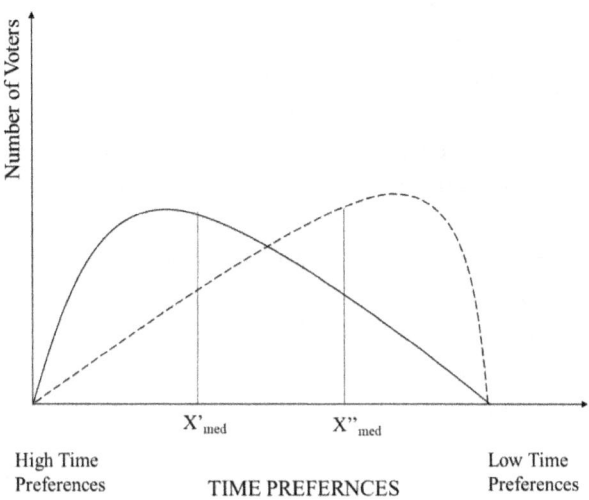

Figure 6-1: Two voter distributions on the time preferences spectrum and the impact on the median voter position.

CAN TIME PREFERENCES BE CHANGED?

Various factors affect people's time preferences. They include "external, biological, personal, and social or institutional ones."[28] Further, time preferences are governed by "forces as habit, self-control, length and certainty of life, regard for offspring and posterity" and can be altered.[29] The major biological factor is the aging process. When a person is a child, s/he will have high time preferences, and this tends to decline as one ages and increases as one nears death. External factors affecting time preference include "property-right security, physical security generally, and observed behavior of others in the community."[30] Religion also affects time preferences. Some religious groups/sects like messianic and

---

28. Hoppe, *Democracy the God That Failed: The Economics and Politics of Monarcy, Democracy, and Natural Order*, 3.

29. Smith, *Time and Public Policy*, 5.

30. Mulligan, *Religion as Adaptation: The Role of Time Preference* 82.

Millenarian sects can encourage high time preferences as they wait for the end of the world and the arrival of their messiah.[31]

Becker and Mulligan also try to understand how people might be able to change their time preferences. They suggest that an individual can change their time preferences by attempting to appreciate future pleasures. Education is one method of lowering time preferences as "through repeated practice at problem-solving, schooling helps children learn the art of scenario simulation. Thus, educated people should be more productive at reducing the remoteness of future pleasures."[32] The family also plays a crucial role in the development of time horizons through the development of trust for outsiders, stress of savings and thrift, discipline, and so on.[33]

However, Banfield suggests these changes are not easy. He states that if a city harbors a substantial lower class, it is virtually impossible to address its most pressing issues fundamentally. Even if good jobs are made available, slums are replaced with better housing, welfare payments are increased, new schools are constructed with a better teacher-student ratio, and more police forces line the streets, one would still have persistent unemployment, housing turning back to slums, schools devolving into chaotic environments with many dropouts, and violent crime still being high.[34]

In essence, the only solution is regeneration. "The issue is not poverty or hunger, but faith and ethics. The present-oriented slave cannot be helped by mere capitalist moralizing about pulling himself up by his own bootstraps- he does not *want* to. Nor will he be helped by handouts-they will only reinforce his moral defects."[35]

---

31. Mulligan, *Religion as Adaptation: The Role of Time Preference* 83.

32. Becker and Mulligan, *The Endogenous Determination of Time Preference*, 736.

33. Smith, *Time and Public Policy*, 25.

34. Banfield, *The Unheavenly City: The Nature and Future of Our Urban Crisis*, 210–11.

35. Chilton, *Productive Christians in an Age of Guilt-Manipulators: A Biblical Response to Ronald J. Sider*, 222.

EMPIRICAL WORK TYING SEXUAL FREEDOM AND TIME PREFERENCES

Some empirical work regarding sexual freedom and time preferences has been completed. One study has found that when men see pretty women, they discount the future more (become present-oriented) as it has to do with mating opportunities.[36] However, it is not clear whether showing cues of pretty women changes underlying time preferences, i.e., do men want to copulate now or are they willing to wait till say marriage to consummate the relationship? The sexual freedom index covering only 21 years, was used to complete empirical analysis to determine the factors impacting sexual freedom. One of the main findings was that citizen ideology (left ideology) is a key factor driving the sexual freedom index. Citizen ideology is tied to time preferences.[37, 38] Right ideology generally shows greater self-control than the left i.e., they have lower time preferences. These seem to be mediated by the role freewill beliefs play for the individual. However, in some instances, those on the left can use external factors to display self-control and achieve results.[39] Left-wing ideology is also a predictor in crime which is an indicator of high time preference, and this could be due to the left's openness to new and exciting experiences whereas those on the right prefer law and order and respect for authority.[40]

An analysis of party platforms for 22 OECD (Organisation for Economic Co-operation and Development) or developed countries found that right parties tended to emphasize more economic freedom versus sexual freedom when compared to left parties. Moreover, post-World War II party platforms for both the right

---

36. Wilson and Daly, *Do Pretty Women Inspire Men to Discount the Future?*, S179.

37. Bose, *The Determinants of Sexual Freedom from 1990 to 2010*, 6.

38. Bose and Jacob, *Changing Sexual Regulations in the U.S. From 1990 to 2010: Spatial Panel Data Analysis*, 1.

39. Clarkson, et al., *The Self-Control Consequences of Political Ideology*, 3.

40. Wright, et al., *Political Ideology Predicts Involvement in Crime*, 5.

and left have started to emphasize sexual freedom. The hypothesis is that parties differ on these issues because left and right parties attract voters with different time preferences. The left parties attract voters with high time preferences (e.g., single mothers, men avoiding fatherhood), whereas the right parties attract voters with low time preferences (e.g., married with children, businessmen), hence party platforms reflect that.[41]

1962 RAT UTOPIA EXPERIMENT AND TIME PREFERENCES

Conducted by John Calhoun in the 1960s, the "Rat Utopia" experiments offer a fascinating glimpse into the potential consequences of a society dominated by high time preferences. In these experiments, rats were provided with unlimited access to food and water within a confined space. They were given everything they needed without any requirement for work or future planning.

Initially, this abundance led to a rapid increase in population. However, this growth was not sustainable and marked the beginning of utopia's decline. As population density increased, the rats began to display a range of unusual behaviors. These included increased aggression, neglect of their young (often leading to their death), withdrawal from social interactions, and a focus on self-beautification.

Interestingly, the rats that focused on beautifying themselves did not engage in breeding or fighting. Their lives were reduced to eating, sleeping, and grooming. This shift in behavior contributed to the decline and eventual extinction of the rat utopia. The birth rate began to collapse, and maladjusted behavior became widespread throughout the colony.[42]

The forced shift to short-term thinking that led to the collapse of the rat utopia has implications for human societies as well. When a society encourages focusing on short-term goals, a variety

---

41. Bose and Van Duyn, *Time Preferences as Partisan Politics: What Do Party Manifestos Show in Twenty-Two Oecd Countries?*, 127–28.

42. Calhoun, *Population Density and Social Pathology*, 139–48.

of problems can follow such as social unrest, neglect of future generations, and a decline in overall societal health.

CONCLUSION

In conclusion, time preferences play an important role in understanding Unwin's thesis. A sexually free society is a society of high time preference individuals, whereas an economically free society is a society of low time preference individuals. For economic growth and prosperity, a society needs to have more individuals with lower time preferences, i.e., people with longer time horizons and increased patience. Various factors affect time preferences, and in the next chapter, we will look at how Christianity, specifically, the Protestant Reformation played a large role in lowering time preferences and lengthening people's time horizons, which becomes instrumental for countries to experience sustained economic growth.

7

Long-Term Thinking in the Bible
and its Impact on Economic Growth and Prosperity

> All Scripture is God-breathed and is useful for teaching, rebuking, correcting and training in righteousness, so that the servant of God may be thoroughly equipped for every good work.
>
> 2 TIM 3:16,17 (NIV)

I SHOWED EARLIER THAT other scholars have found that the Protestant Reformation has been linked to the work ethic (Weber), social ethic (Arruñada), extending time thrift, time discipline, and time sense (Thompson), reevaluation of the bourgeois (McCloskey and Carden), strict Pauline absolute monogamy (Unwin), and European Marriage Pattern (Hajnal). These authors have shown all these factors to be important for sustained economic growth and development (see Chapter 5). Did the Protestant Reformation, focusing on universal literacy to promote Bible reading in the native language, lead to the internalization of new norms that facilitated sustained economic growth? If so, what were these norms?

In this chapter, I will present case studies from the Bible, focusing particularly on the norms found in Genesis. I will then delve into discussions on sexual ethics, tithing, millennialism, and other related topics. Throughout this chapter, I explain that the expectations and behaviors taught in scripture which were to be internalized by Christians, resulted in a lengthening of time horizons, increased commitment to deferred gratification, increased self-discipline, and patience for future gains. This paved the way for sustained economic growth and development.

CASE 1: ADAM & EVE AND THE SIN OF IMPATIENCE

Starting with the first story in the Bible, we see the importance of patience and delaying our gratification. Original sin deals with impatience. God created Adam on day 6 of creation week, the first human. God shaped Adam from the dust of the earth and breathed life into him, marking the beginning of human existence.

God placed Adam in the Garden in Eden, where there was a variety of trees bearing fruits. God gave Adam a command. He told Adam, "You are free to eat from any tree in the garden, but you must not eat from the tree of the knowledge of good and evil, for when you eat from it you will certainly die." (Genesis 2:16,17, NIV). This command was unequivocal, setting a boundary for Adam's actions.

While Adam was in a deep sleep, God performed another act of creation. He took a rib from Adam and fashioned Eve, the first woman. Adam was no longer alone; he had a companion, a helpmate. God then gave them both a command, saying, "I give you every seed-bearing plant on the face of the whole earth and every tree that has fruit with seed in it. They will be yours for food." (Genesis 1:29, NIV). This command was a blessing, granting them dominion over the earth and its produce.

However, a question arises when we consider these two chapters of Genesis together. In Genesis 1:29, God seems to allow them to eat from every tree, but in Genesis 2:16–17, God specifically forbids Adam from eating from the Tree of Knowledge of Good and Evil. Is this a contradiction?

In Genesis 1, God addresses both Adam and Eve, granting them the ability to eat from all the seed-bearing plants and fruit trees. However, in Genesis 2, God specifically instructs only Adam not to eat from the Tree of Knowledge of Good and Evil, warning that doing so would result in death. This apparent contradiction can be resolved by interpreting the prohibition as a temporary measure. In this view, Adam and Eve would eventually be permitted to eat from every tree, including the Tree of Knowledge of Good and Evil. It also suggests that Eve learned about this temporary prohibition from Adam, not directly from God. Thus, the eventual consumption of the fruit from the Tree of Knowledge of Good and Evil, leading to their death, was part of God's plan. This interpretation reconciles the two accounts, providing a coherent narrative of the events in the Garden of Eden.[1]

Why did they have to wait to eat from the Tree of Knowledge of Good and Evil? From Hebrews 5:11 to 14 (NIV), we learn that the knowledge of Good and Evil means wisdom to pass judgment which comes with years of training and experience:[2]

> We have much to say about this, but it is hard to make it clear to you because you no longer try to understand. In fact, though by this time you ought to be teachers, you need someone to teach you the elementary truths of God's word all over again. You need milk, not solid food! Anyone who lives on milk, being still an infant, is not acquainted with the teaching about righteousness. But solid food is for the **mature**, who by constant use have **trained themselves to distinguish good from evil** (emphasis added).

Further, in I Kings 3:9 (NIV) Solomon at the beginning of his reign prays to God: "So give your servant a discerning heart to govern your people and to distinguish between right and wrong. For who is able to govern this great people of yours?" The ability to discern between good and evil (right and wrong) is a fundamental aspect of judgment, a characteristic of good kings and inherently

1. Jordan, *Part 2: From Children to Adults* 15–17 min.
2. Jordan, *Primeval Saints*, 63.

associated with God. However, this ability is not universal. Infants do not possess this ability (Deuteronomy 1:39), and the elderly may lose it due to senility (2 Samuel 19:35).³

In the Genesis narrative, we see that God evaluates His creation, deeming it "good" multiple times. However, when Adam is found to be alone, God declares it 'not good', leading to the creation of Eve, after which God proclaims creation to be "very good" (Genesis 1:31).

Adam and Eve, despite being in adult bodies, are akin to infants in their understanding of the world around them. They are described as "naked and were not ashamed" (Gen 2:25, ESV), signifying their innocence and immaturity.⁴

As adults, it is expected that one should be able to distinguish between good and evil. However, like children, Adam and Eve needed to learn this distinction. The question that arises is whether they were willing to learn gradually or if they sought to expedite the process. This leads us to two distinct interpretations of this matter. The standard interpretation views Adam and Eve's actions as disobedience towards God's command not to eat from the Tree of the Knowledge of Good and Evil. However, a more complete understanding suggests that their sin was not just disobedience, but also **impatience.** They seized something prematurely that God had intended for them to receive later. This interpretation provides a better understanding of the events in the Garden of Eden. God wanted humankind to develop patience and a future orientation.

The temptation of the serpent was a masterclass in manipulation. The serpent exploited their naivety. "You are naked," it hissed, "but one day, you will don the robes of judgment. God has permitted you to eat from every tree, so why hesitate? How long does He expect you to wait? Is it His desire for you to grow older, to gain

---

3. Jordan, *Part 2: From Children to Adults* 28–30 min.

4. It is a common misinterpretation to assume that humanity's original state of nakedness was intended to be permanent, and that clothing was introduced merely to cover sin. In contrast, God is consistently depicted as being clothed, clothed in a garb of light (Psalm 104:2).

wisdom before you partake? Don't fret, Adam isn't stopping you, there's no need to seek his consent."

God honored man's decision immediately. However, Adam and Eve soon discovered the harsh reality—the serpent had lied about the promise of wisdom. They held positions of authority but lacked the maturity to wield it. They found themselves in a predicament they were ill-equipped to handle.

They were devoid of wisdom, yet now they were expected to judge. God had called upon them to judge, but they faltered as they lacked the wisdom. They twisted the truth, calling evil good and good evil (Isaiah 5:20). Instead of accepting their mistakes, they blamed each other and even God (Genesis 3:12,13). Their failure to guard the garden led to their expulsion, and cherubim were appointed to protect it henceforth (Genesis 3:24).

The failure of Adam and Eve in the garden implies that the Bible is about restoration with the new Adam, Jesus Christ. If our original parents' sin was impatience, then we can expect Scripture to teach about the importance of patience, self-control, long-suffering, wisdom, judgment, and so on. We immediately see in the book of Genesis various stories of the patriarchs in whom God developed patience, longer time horizons, and multigenerational thinking. This culminates in the story of Joseph, whom Pharaoh declared the **wisest** man in his realm, appointing him as the second ruler, just below himself (Genesis 41:39–40).[5]

CASE 2: THE PATIENCE AND IMPATIENCE OF ABRAHAM

The recipients of the letter of Hebrews knew that Jesus had conquered Satan and was the King of the world and were wondering why not all things were under his feet (Heb 2:8 (ESV) "'... putting everything in subjection under his feet.' Now in putting everything in subjection to him, he left nothing outside his control. At present, we do not yet see everything in subjection to him.") For this

---

5. Jordan, *Part 3: The Bible Is a Story*, 47–51.

Hebrews 6:12-15 states that the saints need to be patient and trust God of working things in His time. The example of Abraham is highlighted for our consideration.[6]

When God called Abram from Ur, He made him several promises. Initially, as recorded in Genesis 12:1-3, Abram was instructed to journey to a new land. Along with this directive, God assured him that he would become a mighty nation and would be renowned.

Upon his arrival in Canaan, Abram was informed that this land was destined for his offspring. Instead of trying to conquer the land, a much quicker route to possession, he erected two altars, one in Shechem and the other in Bethel, as documented in Genesis 12:6-8. The act of establishing these altars signified his claim to the land in the name of the true God. These altars served not only as places for personal worship but also as sites for corporate worship for those who would convert to his faith.[7]

Genesis 12:5 (KJV) further reveals that Abram brought many souls with him from Haran. The phrase "gotten souls" has been interpreted by commentators as "make souls,"[8] indicating that these individuals were not purchased but converted, thus suggesting an act of evangelization. Moreover, the phrase "called on the name of the Lord" in Genesis 12:8 can also be interpreted as "proclaimed" according to Strong's Concordance.[9] This suggests that while God had promised Abram the land, Abram chose to evangelize it: a process that was slower and requiring more patience than outright conquest, but which ultimately aimed at making the land his own.

Moreover, during the conflict between Chedorlaomer and the Canaanite kings, the latter were defeated and Lot his nephew was captured. Abram and his trained servants, managed to rescue Lot and save the Canaanite kings. Despite his advantageous position, Abram refrained from asserting his dominance over

6. Jordan, *Primeval Saints*, 61.
7. Jordan, *Primeval Saints*, 64.
8. Strong's 6213: To do, make.
9. Strong's 7121: To call, proclaim.

Canaan, choosing instead to wait for the Lord to act. Fearing Chedorlaomer's return, Abram found comfort in God's assurance of protection (Genesis 15:1). God further revealed to Abram that his descendants would inherit the land (Genesis 15:4), a prophecy that was to be fulfilled in the distant future (four hundred years) following a period of exile (Genesis 15:13).

Abram, whose name means "exalted father," demonstrated both patience and impatience in his life. His wife, Sarai, meaning "my princess," was unable to bear children. When God promised that Abram's descendants would inherit the land, Abram and Sarai, in their impatience, decided to take matters into their own hands. She offered Hagar, her maidservant, as a surrogate mother, hoping to fulfill God's promise through her.

This decision reflected their impatience, as Sarai had hoped to adopt the child born of Hagar. However, Hagar did not seem interested in surrendering her child to Sarai. As Ishmael, the son of Hagar and Abram, neared puberty, God appeared to Abram once again (Genesis 16:16 and 17:1–8, 15–16). He told Abram that the promised heir would be born through Sarai, not Hagar.

In recognition of this renewed promise, God changed Abram's name to Abraham, which means "father of a multitude."

Abraham's kids were to inherit the land after 400 years. This would mean that Abraham would have to train his children who would train their children and so on.

> He would have to teach them the word of God. He would have to establish sound patterns, habits, and rituals for them. And he would have to be near to them, comforting them so that they might learn to comfort others. In short, he would have to be a pastor to his family and set up patterns of life that would carry down through the generations. Such long-term, patient endurance in well-doing would, he knew, be rewarded.[10]

Abraham's faith in God's promise was unwavering, as he foresaw its fulfillment in his son Isaac. Even when God commanded him to sacrifice Isaac, Abraham believed that God would

---

10. Jordan, *Primeval Saints*, 69.

restore his son to him (Genesis 22:5 NIV states, "we will come back to you"). Further, in Genesis 21:33, we find an intriguing detail about Abraham planting a tamarisk tree in Beersheba, a dry region on Israel's southern boundary. The tamarisk, an evergreen tree, grows about an inch per year and takes 400 years to reach its full height. Abraham's long-term vision considered his descendants, who would one day emerge from Egypt and benefit from the shade and sustenance provided by the tree, even though he would not enjoy it.[11]

Intriguingly, following Sarah's death, Abraham remarried Keturah and fathered six sons. Each of these sons went on to become the founder of many nations (Genesis 25:1–6), demonstrating the manifestation of God's fulfillment of blessings upon Abraham ("father of a multitude").

The Abraham narrative underscores his unwavering faith and commitment to God's promises, even in the face of adversity. His actions set a precedent for future generations, demonstrating the power of faith, patience, and perseverance in awaiting the fulfillment of God's promises. As Hebrews chapter six states, his life serves as a testament to the power of faith and patience in waiting for the fulfillment of divine promises

CASE 3: JACOB'S CLEAR VISION OF THE FUTURE AND PRESENT-MINDED ESAU

An example in Genesis of the contrast between long-term and short-term perspectives can be found in the story of Jacob and Esau, the twin sons of Isaac. This narrative, recorded in the Bible, showcases a pivotal exchange between two brothers.

Esau, driven by hunger, approached Jacob, falsely claiming to be on the brink of starvation. Jacob, in return for a bowl of stew, demanded something that Esau legally owned as the elder twin—the birthright. Esau could have declined the offer and easily asked

---

11. Schultz, *The Tamarisk Tree*, 4th to 9th paragraph.

any of the many servants who may have already been cooking or who could have cooked something in short order for Esau.

The birthright was not just about receiving a double portion of the father's estate; it also entailed greater responsibility for the care of the parents in their old age. Despite this, Esau readily bartered his birthright for the immediate satisfaction of his hunger, as detailed in Genesis 25:29–34.

Esau got exactly what he desired—a bowl of stew, while Jacob obtained what he sought—the birthright. Esau's focus was intensely on the present. He valued the future so lightly that he was willing to relinquish the unique privilege of the birthright just to satisfy his hunger. Jacob may have seemed unremarkable but possessed a clear vision of the future.

CASE 4: MARRIAGE IN THE BIBLE (PAULINE ABSOLUTE MONOGAMY)

"Let marriage be held in honor among all, and let the marriage bed be undefiled, for God will judge the sexually immoral and adulterous."

HEBREWS 13:4 (ESV)

IN THE AREA OF marriage and sexuality, Christianity limits sexual activity to a man and women within marriage. We see that Paul is writing about the requirements of the Christian sexual ethic in contrast to acceptable pagan norms. Unwin called Paul's teachings Pauline absolute monogamy. The distinctiveness of early Christians had a profound influence on various aspects of Roman society, including practices such as the exposure of infants, gladiatorial games, and other public spectacles. However, the focus here is primarily on the distinctive behaviors related to sexual conduct, that set Christians apart from their pagan Roman contemporaries. We will also see that restricting sex to marriage changed people to think long-term.

I THESSALONIANS—RESTRICTING MEN'S SEXUAL ACTIVITY TO THEIR WIFE

In his first letter to the Thessalonians chapter 4 verse 3, Paul emphasizes the importance of sanctification, i.e., the process of making holy. He explicitly states that God's will for the Thessalonians is their sanctification, which he especially means as an injunction against sexual immorality.[12]

Paul's teachings underscore the expectation that followers, particularly men, should exercise self-control and uphold the sanctity of their bodies (I Thessalonians 4:4–6[13]). This emphasis on sexual purity and restraint was a significant departure from the more permissive attitudes prevalent in Roman society, which highlighted the distinctiveness of Christian ethics and behavior.

In the ancient Greek, the term πορνείας (*porneias*) was primarily used to denote prostitution. However, in his letters, Paul expands the meaning of this term to encompass a wide range of extramarital sexual activities, including sexual relations with slaves, prostitutes, and courtesans, and acts of adultery. Further, the word "vessel" (σκεῦος—*skeuos*) in verse 4 is likely a metaphor referring to a man's wife. In Roman times, a double standard existed regarding sexual morality. Wives were expected to maintain their chastity, while husbands and single men were permitted a certain degree of sexual freedom, particularly with women of lower social status such as slaves, as well as slave men and boys.

Paul's exhortations are primarily directed towards men, challenging the prevailing Roman cultural norms. Paul commands men to restrict their sexual activities to their wives, treating them with honor and respect, not merely as vessels for procreation, but also as partners in marital intimacy.

---

12. "For this is the will of God, your sanctification: that you should abstain from sexual immorality" NKJV.

13. "that each of you should know how to possess his own vessel in sanctification and honor, not in passion of lust, like the Gentiles who do not know God; that no one should take advantage of and defraud his brother in this matter, because the Lord *is* the avenger of all such, as we also forewarned you and testified." NKJV.

Following this, Paul discusses the concept of brotherly love, a virtue that the Thessalonians were already practicing (vs. 9). In chapter 4, verses 11 and 12,[14] he introduces the idea of a **forward-looking** work ethic. He suggests that once the domestic life, particularly the sexual ethic, is in order, that Christians can begin to develop a future-oriented perspective through work, thrift, foresight, and the exercise of dominion. This teaching represents a significant departure from the prevailing societal norms and extends time horizons of families and societies.

I CORINTHIANS—DISCIPLINING SINFUL SEXUAL BEHAVIOR

In the first epistle to the Corinthians, Paul addresses the issue of sexual purity, a theme that resonates throughout his teachings. In the fifth chapter of this epistle, he again deals with the issue of *porneia*, a term for him that encompasses various forms of sexual immorality.

A particular case had arisen in the Corinthian church where a man was engaged in a sexual relationship with his father's wife, likely his stepmother, who was presumably much younger than his father. This was a clear violation of the moral and sexual standards that Paul had set for the Christian community that even the Gentiles acknowledged as wrong. Despite the gravity of the situation, the church seemed to have turned a blind eye to this transgression.[15]

Paul, in his wisdom and authority, urged the church to take decisive action. He recommended that they deliver the man "to Satan for the destruction of the flesh, that his spirit may be saved" (NKJV). This was a call for the church to exercise discipline over

---

14. "that you also aspire to lead a quiet life, to mind your own business, and to work with your own hands, as we commanded you, that you may walk properly toward those who are outside, and *that* you may lack nothing." (NKJV).

15. Hurtado, *Destroyer of the Gods: Early Christian Distinctiveness in the Roman World*, 161.

its members, ensuring that they adhered to the prescribed sexual behaviors.

Also, in the sixth chapter of the first letter to Corinthians, verses 9–10, Paul issues a stern warning against a range of activities, including various forms of sexual behaviors such as adultery, homosexuality, fornication, and sodomy. He emphasizes that such behaviors are incompatible with inheriting the Kingdom of God. In economic terms, behaviors such as adultery (focused on immediate pleasure regardless of family consequences), homosexuality and sodomy (sterile relationships that don't produce offspring), and fornication (showing impatience and lack of self-control) are all high time preference activities (short time horizons) and are condemned by Paul.

I CORINTHIANS—BANNING SEXUAL RELATIONS WITH PROSTITUTES AND BECOMING ONE FLESH

Further, in First Corinthians chapter 6 verses 12–20, Paul addresses the issue of men engaging in sexual relations with prostitutes, a practice that was deemed acceptable in pagan Roman society. The Christian men justified their actions with slogans, likely not originating from Paul, such as "all things are lawful for me" and "foods for the stomach and the stomach for foods."[16]

Paul counters these justifications, asserting, "I will not be brought under the power of any" and "Now the body is not for sexual immorality [*porneia*] but for the Lord, and the Lord for the body." He underscores the sanctity of the human body, stating that our bodies are "members of Christ"; sexual relations with prostitutes are therefore strictly forbidden.

Paul further elaborates that during sexual intercourse, the two individuals "become one flesh." He reminds the Corinthians that their bodies are the "temple of the Holy Spirit who is in you,

---

16. The New Revised Standard Version and other versions have these in quotes.

whom you have from God" (NKJV). Given that they were purchased at the price of Jesus' death, they are obligated to glorify God in both body and spirit. This serves as a powerful reminder of the Christian duty to uphold sexual purity and holiness.

As stated earlier, the term *porneia* was not used to describe all extramarital sexual activity, but by Paul using this term to describe these activities, he labels these activities as sinful and not appropriate for Christians to engage in. "In doing so . . . , he asserted and reflected a stance diametrically opposed to the prevailing attitudes of the time, and he intended to distinguish sharply what should be the sexual behavior of believers, particularly males."[17]

In the fifteenth chapter of the first epistle to the Corinthians, Paul delves into the concept of Jesus' resurrection of the body, presenting it as a model for believers. He emphasizes that our mortal bodies are destined for transformation in the future, a shift from a present-oriented focus on pleasure and short-term gratification. This **future-oriented perspective** is a recurring theme in the Bible, encouraging believers to look beyond the immediate and consider the future. Consideration of the future extends time horizons and is important for economic growth and prosperity.

I CORINTHIANS—AVOIDING SEXUAL ASCETICISM WITHIN MARRIAGE

In the seventh chapter of I Corinthians, verses 1–16, Paul addresses a slogan related to sexual asceticism (verse 1): "It is good for a man not to touch [sexually] a woman" (NKJV). This slogan appears to advocate for asceticism within marriage. However, Paul counters this notion with a robust endorsement of sexual relations within the confines of marriage.

While Paul condemns sexual relations with prostitutes in the sixth chapter, here he strongly advocates for marital sex. He posits that sex within marriage can serve as a deterrent for believers against engaging in illicit sexual activities. He underscores the

---

17. Hurtado, *Destroyer of the Gods: Early Christian Distinctiveness in the Roman World*, 163.

importance of mutual respect between husbands and wives, particularly regarding their conjugal rights. He warns against deprivation (*apostereo*), meaning defrauding or stealing from one another, between husband and wife.

In verse 2[18] of the seventh chapter, Paul uses the term '*porneias*' in the plural form to refer to sexual fornications. He emphasizes the significance of marital sex to avoid all types of '*porneias*' or various illegal sexual activities ("sexual immorality"). He stipulates that the only permissible avoidance of sexual activity with one's spouse should be by mutual agreement and for a limited duration, provided that this time is dedicated to prayer.

The use of '*porneias*' in plural form indicates that any sexual activity outside of marriage with one's spouse is strictly prohibited. Paul suggests that marital sex serves as a "*hedge against these various temptations to extramarital sex of any kind.*"[19] (italics in original). This perspective marks a significant departure from the prevailing Roman attitudes of the time, underscoring the transformative power of Christian teachings on sexual morality and emphasizing the importance of Pauline absolute monogamy.

I TIMOTHY—NOT HAVING SEXUAL DOUBLE STANDARDS

Paul's teachings in the New Testament often addressed the prevailing double standards between men and women, particularly in the context of leadership within the Church. During the Roman era, the phrase "wife of one husband" was lauded as a virtue. Both Greek and Latin languages had specific terms to praise women who demonstrated loyalty to their husbands. They were '*monandros*' in Greek and '*univira*' in Latin.

In the first letter to Timothy chapter five, verse 9, Paul stipulates that deserving widows who were to receive support from the

---

18. "Nevertheless, because of sexual immorality, let each man have his own wife, and let each woman have her own husband." (NKJV).

19. Hurtado, *Destroyer of the Gods: Early Christian Distinctiveness in the Roman World*, 165.

Church should be the "wife of one husband" (ESV). This was a clear endorsement of marital fidelity among women.

However, Paul extends this requirement of sexual loyalty to men as well, marking a significant shift in societal norms. In the same epistle, chapter 3, verses 2 and 12, he states that a bishop or overseer and deacons should be the "husband of one wife." This was a radical departure from the prevailing double standards, demanding the same level of commitment and loyalty from men that was expected of women.

Interestingly, there were no equivalent terms in Latin and Greek for *'univira'* and *'monandros'* that applied to men. To address this, Paul coined a new term: *'mias gynaikos andra,'* which translates to 'husband of one wife.'[20]

This shift in expectations brought men to the same standard as women, significantly altering the dynamics within the family structure. Men were now held to the same standards of loyalty and commitment as women. This enabled the synchronization of time preferences, significantly enhancing the family's ability to act as a unified entity with a shared future orientation allowing for the effective taking of dominion. This also reduces conflicts when there is a mismatch in time preferences and further it also extends time horizons especially when children and grandchildren are involved. As children are the projection of the family into the future, they will carry on the family name and Christian capital into the future (Psalm 127:4–5).

CASE 5: SEXUAL ABUSE OF CHILDREN

During the Roman era, the sexual exploitation of children, including very young ones, was not only tolerated but also celebrated by contemporary writers. This disturbing practice was not condemned, reflecting the societal norms of the time. However, with the advent of Christianity, a stark contrast emerged in attitudes towards such heinous acts.

20. Hurtado, *Destroyer of the Gods: Early Christian Distinctiveness in the Roman World*, 166.

Christian teachings unequivocally condemned the sexual abuse and corruption of children. Early Christian texts, such as the *Didache* and the *Epistle of Barnabas*, explicitly denounced the corruption of children. The term "pederasty," from the Greek *paiderasteia*, which referred to sexual relationships between adult men and boys, was redefined by Christians as child sexual corruption.

Numerous early Christian writers sought to highlight the moral decay and depravity of the pagan world as part of their apologetic strategy. They countered the arguments put forth by pagan writers against Christianity by emphasizing the contrast in moral standards. Athenagoras, in his defense of Christianity, condemned homosexual conduct, including relationships between men and boys.

> For those who have set up a market for fornication, and established infamous resorts for the young for every kind of vile pleasure,—who do not abstain even from males, males with males committing shocking abominations, outraging all the noblest and comeliest bodies in all sorts of ways, so dishonouring the fair workmanship of God . . . these men, I say, revile us for the very things which they are conscious of themselves, and ascribe to their own gods, boasting of them as noble deeds, and worthy of gods. These adulterers and paederasts defame the eunuchs and the once-married.[21]

Pederasty was considered a grave sin in early Christian teachings, so much so that it warranted exclusion from the Christian community. While early Christian teachings also extolled celibacy, it is clear from the scriptures that the Christian ideal of sex was to be between a man and a woman, and within the marriage covenant. Any deviation from this was strongly discouraged.

Christian theology was distinct and unambiguous in its condemnation of sexual relations between adults and children, a notable departure from Greco-Roman thought. This Christian sexual ethic led to a significant decline in sexual encounters between

---

21. Bakke, *When Children Became People: The Birth of Childhood in Early Christianity*, 141.

adults and children, demonstrating the transformative power of these teachings.

Why is this important. Many corrupted children suffer various problems later in life. These include psychological consequences (depression, anxiety, eating disorders, etc.), physical consequences (obesity, poorer overall health, gynecological issues, etc.), psychosocial impacts (promiscuity, adultery, divorce, etc.,), and socioeconomic consequences (less college, less income, higher unemployment etc.,).[22] Many of these consequences are correlated with higher time preferences and hence present orientation. Protecting children from predators increases the future orientation of society.

CASE 6: TITUS: SELF-CONTROL FOR ALL

While limiting sexual relations to between married people, other teachings in the Bible also focus on extending time horizons and lowering time preferences, thus impacting prosperity.

In the second chapter of Titus, the Apostle Paul provides explicit and implicit guidance on the issue of self-control to five distinct groups within the Christian community. This virtue is emphasized as a central tenet of Christian life, regardless of one's age or social status.

- Older Men (Verse 2): Paul advises older men to be sober-minded. He also encourages them to be self-controlled, demonstrating discipline and not being driven by their passions. This guidance underscores the importance of wisdom and restraint that comes with age and experience.

- Older Women (Verse 3): Older women are advised to be careful in their speech, particularly when speaking about others who are not present, thus avoiding slander. They are warned against becoming slaves to wine, emphasizing the importance of self-control and freedom from substance dependency.

---

22. Jeglic, *The Long-Lasting Consequences of Child Sexual Abuse*, all.

Further, older women are urged to guide or impart lessons of prudence and self-control to younger women.

- Younger Women (Verses 4–5): Younger women are encouraged to be self-controlled and not driven by their passions. They are to love their husbands and children emphasizing the importance of family. It underscores the importance of maintaining personal integrity and moral discipline.
- Younger Men (Verses 6–8): Younger men are advised to be self-controlled and disciplined, not driven by passions for wealth, fame, sex, power, or success. This counsel is particularly pertinent given the societal pressures younger men may face to achieve success and recognition.
- Slaves (Verses 9–10): While the term "self-control" is not explicitly used in Paul's instructions to slaves, the characteristics he describes—honesty, trustworthiness, and a good attitude—are indicative of a self-controlled life. Slaves are advised against pilfering and encouraged to demonstrate good faith, showing that they can be trusted.

Throughout this chapter, Paul uses the term *"sophronas,"* which means "self-controlled" to emphasize the importance of self-control and patience in the Christian life. This term appears in various forms in his addresses to older men, older women, younger women, and younger men. Even in his instructions to slaves, where the term is not explicitly used, the principle of self-control is assumed. This consistent emphasis on self-control across all groups demonstrates that sensible, self-controlled behavior is a distinguishing component of the Christian life and has a significant influence on all types of relationships to create a future-oriented Christian community which is important for economic growth and prosperity.[23]

---

23. Media, *Leader's Guide, Session 4: Titus 2:1–10*, 2–4.

CASE 7: TITHING AND FUTURE ORIENTATION

> Will a man rob God? Yet ye have robbed me. But ye say, Wherein have we robbed thee? In tithes and offerings. Ye are cursed with a curse: for ye have robbed me, even this whole nation. Bring ye all the tithes into the storehouse, that there may be meat in mine house, and prove me now herewith, saith the Lord of hosts, if I will not open you the windows of heaven, and pour you out a blessing, that there shall not be room enough to receive it. (Malachi 3:9–10) (KJV)

Conducted by Shah, a study on the impact of tithing (giving 10% of your income away), revealed transformative effects among the poorest populations in India, Peru, and South Sudan. The research focused on how religious faith influences the financial habits of these communities.

The study found that the poor in India often spend their discretionary income on immediate gratifications such as alcohol, tobacco, and festivals, rather than saving or investing for the future. Shah suggests that this tendency could be attributed to a lack of self-control, which might be a significant factor that leads the poor to sacrifice their "future to gain a shortlived and less optimal reward in the present."[24]

Some theorists propose that poverty itself erodes self-control, creating a circular argument. However, Shah's research offers a different perspective when it comes to the practice of tithing among the poor.

When credit was extended to the poor, Shah observed that those who practiced tithing—the act of giving a significant portion of one's income, typically 10%, to God—were more likely to invest these funds into assets that yield future returns, rather than spending on immediate needs.

This practice of tithing cultivates a culture of self-restraint, of "innerworldly asceticism," as Shah puts it. It acts as a protective

---

24. Shah, *Religion and Economic Empowerment among the Enterprising Poor*, 44.

shield, preventing the poor from falling into the trap of myopic over-consumption.[25] Thus, tithing as a Christian practice, emerges as a powerful tool that can potentially transform the financial behaviors of the poor and others, encouraging long-term planning and investment, hence impacting economic growth and prosperity.

CASE 8: MILLENNIALISM AND TIME PREFERENCE

The perspective on the future holds significant importance, especially in the context of end-times theology. There are three primary millennial schools of thought in Christianity: Premillennialism, Postmillennialism, and Amillennialism. Each presents a distinct view of the future. Postmillennialists, with their optimistic outlook, tend to have longer time horizons. In contrast, Premillennialists, who anticipate the imminent return of Jesus Christ, have a more short-term oriented perspective and are also pessimistic about the future. Amillennialism is between these two possibilities.

A research paper by McCleary and Barro explores the impact of various branches of Protestant missions in Guatemala, particularly on human capital accumulation. They distinguished between mainline Protestants, Evangelicals, and Pentecostal groups, the latter two of which they categorized as premillennialists. The latter groups focused on the impending return of Christ to establish His earthly reign, which led them to de-emphasize institution-building and investments in areas like education, medicine, and law.

On the other hand, mainline Protestants prioritized civilization building. This included establishing educational institutions, translating Bibles into native languages, launching literacy campaigns, and more. Their approach was focused on long-term societal development as their millennial views were different from the evangelicals and Pentecostals.[26]

---

25. Shah, *Religion and Economic Empowerment among the Enterprising Poor*, 45.

26. McCleary and Barro, *Protestants and Catholics and Educational Investment in Guatemala*, 169.

McCleary and Barro's study revealed that mainline Protestant schools have a more significant impact on enhancing literacy than other Protestant schools. This finding underscores the influence of theological beliefs regarding the millennium on societal development and the importance of longer time horizons.

CASE 9: OTHER AREAS OF FUTURE ORIENTATION

The biblical faith is future-oriented. There are numerous other areas of teaching in the Bible that deal with lowering time preferences. These include the teachings on the fruits of the spirit (Galatians 5:22–23), with three of them dealing with the issue of time (patience, faithfulness, self-control). Further numerous commandments from the Ten Commandments teach self-control and are time preference related. For example, the tenth commandment teaches one not to covet. Christianity prohibited envy and jealousy. Men are not to covet their neighbor's goods (Exodus 20:17), nor are they to envy the prosperity of the wicked (Proverbs 24:19–20).

The Social Gospel advocates for wealth redistribution by the government to assist the less fortunate. However, employing the government in such a manner is seen as a breach of both the eight and tenth commandments. Using wealth redistribution tends to shorten time horizons.

In 1966, Helmut Schoeck conducted a comprehensive and scholarly analysis of envy, which he documented in his book titled "Envy." Schoeck distinguishes between envy and jealousy. Jealousy involves a desire to possess something that rightfully belongs to someone else. A jealous individual anticipates gaining from acquiring what the other person owns someone like a thief. Envy, on the other hand, is far more subtle and harmful. Envy is not about elevating oneself by emulating the person of wealth, but to see the other person brought down. In cultures characterized by envy, individuals are more likely to empathize with another's misfortune and less inclined to celebrate their success. Further, there is a fear of success in such cultures as people are afraid of attracting the "evil eye."[27] Envy was seen as one of the medieval church's seven deadly sins which the church preached against and contributed to economic growth.

Even fruit tree regulations mandated that no fruits be harvested during the first three years. In the fourth year, the entire crop was to be dedicated to the Lord, and only in the fifth year could the fruits be eaten (Leviticus 19:23–25). This practice underscores the importance of developing patience.

Even more could be said in the areas of taking sabbaths and sabbatical rests. Scripture is full of prophecies that incline the believer to the future (e.g., looking for the promised messiah), and sometimes the future beyond one's lifetime. Even in the mission field, many successful missionaries went out in the hopes of a better future and changing history, which they did in various ways.[28] They often went out against great odds. This requires an ability to imagine a future that does not yet exist.

CONCLUSION

In conclusion, the Bible teaches that male sexuality is manageable and should be confined within the family. It advocates for self-discipline, sobriety, and hence extending time horizons. While Unwin theorized that women's restraint of their sex life was the key to civilization building, the teachings of Paul were focused on men exercising restraint. The responsibility for transgressions such as adultery, rape, and fornication are primarily placed on men. It encourages self-restraint, maturity, and self-control. If lust is not managed, it hinders the ability to make long-term commitments. However, when men abandon immature behaviors, they can undertake more significant endeavors by investing, constructing, establishing institutions, exploring, and innovating. That is expanding time horizons because of lowered time preferences. In other areas of scripture, we also see the push for future orientation.

---

27. Schoeck, *Envy: A Theory of Social Behavior*, 57–76.
28. Woodberry, *The Missionary Roots of Liberal Democracy*, 244–74.

The Reformation emphasized Bible reading and broader educational goals, which resulted in the dissemination and standardization of religious beliefs that geared the mindset to long-term thinking and expanded the social circle where exchange occurs. Regularly reading, meditating, and applying what is in the Bible enables one to fulfill Paul's teaching in Romans 12:2, where he explains that renewing our minds through scripture leads to our **transformation**. The instillation of these social norms emphasized self-restraint, a sense of time, an awareness of past and future, and an expanded sense of dominion all resulting in growth and maturity of the individual and society. This ties in with Unwin's observation that civilizations that adopted Pauline absolute monogamy were expansive. Pauline absolute monogamy and its civilizing process occurred only with the Reformation.[29]

> [M]onogamous marriage shifts men's psychology in ways that tend to reduce crime, violence, and zero-sum thinking while promoting broader trust, long-term investments, and steady economic accumulation. Rather than pursuing impulsive or risky behaviors aimed at catapulting themselves up the social ladder, low-status men in monogamous societies have a chance to marry, have children, and invest in the future. High-status men can and will still compete for status, but the currency of that competition can no longer involve the accumulation of wives or concubines.[30]

Catholicism faced challenges in widely instilling this norm because it did not encourage Bible reading in the native language, instead focusing on the elites. While there were precursors to capitalism in Northern Italy Pre-Reformation, it was insufficient for sustained economic growth. Islam failed to produce sustained economic growth, as it did not require men to exercise self-control in the area of sexuality by allowing polygamy (polygyny). The male sexual lust was seen as a fact of life and nothing could be

---

29. Elias, *The Civilizing Process: The History of Manners*, 183.

30. Henrich, *The Weirdest People in the World: How the West Became Psychologically Peculiar and Particularly Prosperous*, 281.

done about it, hence women's clothing had to be in a way for her to guard her chastity and avoid sexual seduction.[31] Polygyny impacts negatively a man's willingness to invest in his wife and children as he seeks other potential wives.[32] Whereas monogamy gives even low-status men a stake in the future by providing a pathway to have and raise children.[33] Future orientation is essential for economic growth and prosperity.

---

31. Though men have also been encouraged to lower their gaze when they see women Surkheel, *The Male Lust, the Female Form and the Forbidden Gaze*, para. 9–11.

32. Polygamy creates various problems. They include the man having to spend equal time and equal resources for each of his wives. Further issues of jealousy, in-laws, child up bringing, and other disputes weakens families.

33. Henrich, *The Weirdest People in the World: How the West Became Psychologically Peculiar and Particularly Prosperous*, 267–68.

8

Sexual Freedom, Guilt, Confession
and Its Impact on Economic growth and Prosperity

"The state of the moral man is one of tranquillity and peace, the state of an immoral man is one of perpetual unrest."

MARQUIS DE SADE

"Thus, a good man, though a slave, is free; but a wicked man, though a king, is a slave. For he serves, not one man alone, but, what is worse, as many masters as he has vices."

SAINT AUGUSTINE

THE BIBLE UNEQUIVOCALLY CONDEMNS sexual immorality, emphasizing that it is not merely an external act but a sin against one's own body (1 Corinthians 6:18).[1,2] When one commits sexual sin,

---

1. "Run away from sexual immorality [in any form, whether thought or behavior, whether visual or written]. Every *other* sin that a man commits is outside the body, but the one who is sexually immoral sins against his own body." I Cor 6:18 (AMP).

2. It is important to note that Paul did not claim sexual immorality to be the worst of all sins, as is sometimes assumed. Rather, he addressed the

guilt inevitably follows, prompting the need for justification and atonement. In this chapter, I will look at how a guilt-filled society, resulting from sexual liberation, impacts economic growth and prosperity. Furthermore, I will examine how intellectuals with guilty consciences, stemming from sexually deviant lifestyles, pursue truth. Understanding their moral lives is crucial to discerning whether they have the broader benefit of society in mind or are primarily self-serving.

RESPONSES TO GUILT AND ITS IMPLICATIONS FOR PROSPERITY

A Christian confesses sin to God and repents and turns to the Lord Jesus Christ. Psalms 32:5 (ESV) captures the essence of confession: "I acknowledged my sin to you, and I did not cover my iniquity; I said, 'I will confess my transgressions to the Lord,' and you forgave the iniquity of my sin." Confession is an acknowledgment of wrongdoing, a humbling act that opens the door to forgiveness. James 5:16 encourages believers to confess their sins to one another, fostering accountability and healing.

Confession is not merely a private matter between an individual and God; it extends to our relationships with fellow humans. Romans 8:1 (NIV) provides immense comfort: "Therefore, there is now no condemnation for those who are in Christ Jesus." God's grace transcends our failings. Through Jesus' sacrificial work on the cross, sin's guilt and shame are removed.

We are created in God's image. For this reason, sin, the breaking of his commandments, affects everyone whether they believe in God or not. For this reason, secularists also experience guilt and seek avenues for confession. Whether it is "coming out" during homosexual pride events or celebrities sharing (confessing) their

---

casual attitude toward sexual sin prevalent among some Christians in hypersexualized cultures. However, sex outside of marriage is considered qualitatively worse than other sins in certain respects because it creates a one-flesh union that uniquely defiles the body. Some proponents of this view also argue that immoral sex is not merely a physical act but has a spiritual dimension as well.

abortion stories, secular confession reflects a universal human need for release from guilt. Many also confess their sin in their works as they seek to rationalize and justify their misbehavior to salve their conscience.

Secularists, like anyone else, grapple with guilt and the need for self-justification and self-atonement. Some engage in masochistic self-atonement. They seek relief through self-destructive behaviors like alcoholism and marrying known alcoholics, gambling knowing the odds are stacked against them, or burden-bearing as forms of self-punishment. The latter involves individuals voluntarily taking on the emotional or practical weight of another person's or group's struggles and becoming public saints to atone for private guilt.[3] Injustice collecting, a form of masochism, involves placing oneself in situations where offense is anticipated. The collector perceives every slight or perceived wrongdoing as a personal affront, casting themselves as the perpetual innocent party. It's as if the universe conspires to target them alone, creating a self-imposed cycle of suffering. In this masochistic dance, the injustice collector clings to their victimhood, accumulating grievances like rare coins. Each offense reinforces their narrative: "This can only happen to me." The weight of perceived injustice becomes their burden, and they carry it willingly, seeking validation in their suffering.[4]

A secularist, burdened by guilt that cannot be absolved through self-atonement, may turn to the state for redemption. This guilt, coupled with a masochistic tendency, can lead to a desire for a form of political servitude. In terms of policy, such a person might advocate for high taxation. This can be seen as a form of self-punishment where success is penalized. They may also favor

---

3. For e.g., Black Lives Matter protests after the George Floyd's death was predominantly done by Whites. Mobilewalla, *New Report Reveals Demographics of Black Lives Matter Protesters Shows Vast Majority Are White, Marched within Their Own Cities*, section 3.

4. Rushdoony, *Politics of Guilt and Pity*, 1–3.

policies that protect criminals at the expense of law-abiding citizens, leading to a degradation of their living conditions.[5]

Sadism, the counterpart to masochism, involves deriving pleasure from inflicting pain, humiliation, or suffering upon others to deal with guilt. Sadists may manipulate situations to shift blame or guilt onto innocent parties. By doing so, they absolve themselves of responsibility. Sadistic individuals seek retribution even when directed at those who have not wronged them, and they may seek to seduce the innocent. For example, they may seduce virgins or faithful wives, regardless of their personal feelings for them. They will seek to corrupt children who are seen as innocent. E.g., we see this in drag events targeting children and we also see many guilt-filled teachers targeting innocent children in public schools by confessing their sexually deviant lifestyles to them.[6] Sadist's actions prioritize conquest, dominance, and inflicting pain. In the biblical story, Cain's jealousy led him to kill his brother Abel. Abel became the scapegoat for Cain's inner turmoil and resentment.[7]

Both masochism and sadism are futile. Sadistic patterns harm others, and masochistic self-punishment fails to address the root of sin, guilt, and shame. When it comes to economic freedom, a society dominated by guilt will desire less of it. The collective guilt and self-punishment lead to a preference for restrictive economic policies, limiting individual success and fostering a culture of failure and irresponsibility. Self-harm also means economic self-harm resulting in less economic freedom. A society that is less free means that it will be less prosperous. A society burdened with guilt cannot truly be free economically.

---

5. Rushdoony, *Politics of Guilt and Pity*, 11–15.

6. Shakeshaft, *Educator Sexual Misconduct: A Synthesis of Existing Literature*, 1–148.

7. Rushdoony, *Politics of Guilt and Pity*, 5, 16.

GUILTY CONSCIOUSNESS AND INTELLECTUAL PURSUIT

Debased sexual actions lead to debased minds as a sort of confession and self-justification. According to Jones, "The intellectual life is a function of the moral life of the thinker. To apprehend truth, which is the goal of the intellectual life, one must live a moral life." He further states that intellectual pursuits can "either conform desire to truth or truth to desire."[8]

To truly apprehend truth, one must live a moral life according to Jones. In other words, our ethical choices and character influence our ability to seek and recognize truth. This implies aligning our desires, inclinations, and preferences with objective truth. On the other hand, guilty consciences involve distorting or bending the truth to fit our desires or preconceived notions to allow for self-justification. Living ethically in the area of sexuality enhances our capacity to apprehend truth.

Romans 1 interestingly links debased sexual actions (sins) with debased minds. This provides credence to Jones' statement about the intellectual life being a function of the moral life.

> For the wrath of God is revealed from heaven against all ungodliness and unrighteousness of men, who by their unrighteousness suppress the truth.... For although they knew God, they did not honor him as God or give thanks to him, but they became futile in their thinking, and their foolish hearts were darkened. Claiming to be wise, they became fools,... Therefore God gave them up in the lusts of their hearts to impurity, to the dishonoring of their bodies among themselves, because they exchanged the truth about God for a lie and worshiped and served the creature rather than the Creator, who is blessed forever! Amen. For this reason God gave them up to dishonorable passions. For their women exchanged natural relations for those that are contrary to nature; and the men likewise gave up natural relations with women and were

---

8. Jones, *Degenerate Moderns: Modernity as Rationalized Sexual Misbehavior*, 15.

consumed with passion for one another, men committing shameless acts with men and receiving in themselves the due penalty for their error. <u>And since they did not see fit to acknowledge God, God gave them up to a debased mind to do what ought not to be done.</u> (Romans 1:18–28 ESV, underline added).

We will now examine a few key intellectuals and analyze whether their guilty consciences resulted in their intellectual pursuits conforming truth to a desire for self-justification, rather than for the benefit of society.

INTELLECTUAL 1: MARGARET MEAD AND UNRAVELING THE CONTROVERSIES OF AN ANTHROPOLOGIST

Margaret Mead, a renowned anthropologist, left an indelible mark on the field with her work. Her 1928 book, *"Coming of Age in Samoa,"* explored the lives of Samoan adolescents and challenged prevailing Western notions of sexuality, fidelity, and family dynamics. "Romantic love as it occurs in our civilisation, inextricably bound up with ideas of monogamy, exclusiveness, jealousy and undeviating fidelity does not occur in Samoa" she observed.[9]

Mead's observations in Samoa revealed a stark contrast to Western norms. Samoan teenagers exhibited uninhibited sexuality, and celibacy held no significance for them. Fidelity was scoffed at, and adultery and divorce were not met with the same gravity as in Western societies. Casual homosexual practices among the youth were also commonplace. Children were raised collectively, emphasizing communal responsibility. Mead's findings challenged the restrictive sexual mores prevalent in Western cultures. She believed that human nature was plastic and adaptable to diverse social contexts.

Anthropologist Derek Freeman later criticized Mead's research, claiming that her findings were fraudulent. He argued that

9. Mead, *Coming of Age in Samoa: A Psychological Study of Primitive Youth for Western Civilization*, 105.

Samoan society idealized female virginity and that pre-Christian Samoa punished adultery with death. Further, Samoa was not a free-sex utopia.[10] Freeman's assertions ignited a heated debate about the authenticity of Mead's work.

Mead's personal life added complexity to her research. She was married to an Episcopalian seminarian but engaged in adultery. In 1925, ostensibly on a trip to New York for a job interview, she met Edward Sapir and spent a night with him. In the same year, she set out to Samoa to do research. During her research trip to Samoa, she had a long-running lesbian relationship with Ruth Benedict. Mead's own experiences may have influenced her interpretations of Samoan sexuality. On her way back from Samoa, she has another adulterous relationship with a shipmate named Fortune. He became the second of her three husbands.[11]

Critics wondered if Mead projected her unrepentant adultery onto Samoan culture. Did her personal choices color her observations? The Samoans "laugh at stories of romantic love, scoff at fidelity . . . believe one love will quickly cure another."[12] Mead's recommendation for Americans to reconsider sexual mores based on her Samoan research raised eyebrows. Was she advocating for greater sexual freedom to challenge cultural norms that were based on Christianity?

Mead's anthropology blurred the lines between objective research and personal beliefs. Was her work an attempt to rationalize her sexual behavior? Was her conscience troubled by sexual sin? Was she seeking self-atonement from her unorthodox relationships and did her fluid approach to fidelity influence her perspective on Samoan society?

---

10. Freeman, *Margaret Mead and Samoa: The Making and Unmaking of an Anthropological Myth*, 236, 41.

11. Jones, *Degenerate Moderns: Modernity as Rationalized Sexual Misbehavior*, 32–35.

12. Mead, *Coming of Age in Samoa: A Psychological Study of Primitive Youth for Western Civilization*, 104–05.

INTELLECTUAL 2: JOHN MAYNARD KEYNES THE FOUNDER OF MACROECONOMICS

John Maynard Keynes and his ideas form the foundation for nearly all macroeconomic policies implemented by our federal government and governments around the world. He viewed Christianity as a force that promotes saving. In his 1929 work, he states that "the morals, the politics, the literature, and the religion of the age [are] joined in a grand conspiracy for the promotion of saving."[13] Further, in his 1949 work, while criticizing the Benthamite (utilitarian) tradition, he was also against Christianity (Puritanism specifically) and stated that Christianity represents "tradition, convention and hocus pocus."[14]

Keynes was known for his "life-long bias against long-run thinking," according to his biographer and economist, Skidelsky. He was not willing to risk too much of the present for the sake of a better future. Hazlitt, in "The Failure of the 'New Economics,'" states, "The great virtue is consumption, extravagance, improvidence. The great vice is saving, thrift, 'financial prudence.'" Keynes himself famously said, "In the long run we are all dead."[15]

His theory provided a justification for deficit spending and encouraged focusing on the short run rather than waiting for the long run to work itself out. Before Keynes, the dominant school was the classical economists. They believed that the economy could achieve the long run quickly hence government intervention was not needed. However, Keynes' ideas were welcomed by politicians who wanted to spend without the constraint of balancing the budget. This made Keynes popular among politicians.

Keynes was against future-oriented people or purposive men as he calls them. He writes in his book, Economic Possibilities for Our Grandchildren:

---

13. Keynes, *A Tract on Monetary Reform*, 7.
14. Keynes, *Two Memoirs*, 96.
15. Hazlitt, *The Failure of the "New Economics": An Analysis of the Keynesian Fallacies*, 127.

Of course there will still be many people with intense, unsatisfied purposiveness who will blindly pursue wealth-unless they can find some plausible substitute. But the rest of us will no longer be under any obligation to applaud and encourage them. For we shall inquire more curiously than is safe to-day into the true character of this "purposiveness" with which in varying degrees Nature has endowed almost all of us. <u>For purposiveness means that we are more concerned with the remote future results of our actions than with their own quality or their immediate effects on our own environment.</u> The <u>"purposive" man is always trying to secure a spurious and delusive immortality for his acts by pushing his interest in them forward into time.</u> He does not love his cat, but his cat's kittens; nor, in truth, the kittens, but only the kittens' kittens, and so on forward forever to the end of cat-dom ... (underline added).[16]

Arguing from the absurd, he argues in the *"The Economic Consequences of the Peace" 1920*

<u>The duty of "saving" became nine-tenths of virtue and the growth of the cake the object of true religion.</u> There grew round the non-consumption of the cake all those instincts of puritanism which in other ages has withdrawn itself from the world and has neglected the arts of production as well as those of enjoyment. And so the cake increased; but to what end was not clearly contemplated. Individuals would be exhorted not so much to abstain as to defer, and to cultivate the pleasures of security and anticipation. Saving was for old age or for your children; but this was only in theory—<u>the virtue of the cake was that it was never to be consumed, neither by you nor by your children after you</u> (underline added).[17]

Further, according to Keynes, a saver was seen as an exploiter. By saving, he "forced another individual to transfer some wealth item to him." Keynes anticipated the "euthanasia" of the

---

16. Keynes, *Economic Possibilities for Our Grandchildren*, 370.
17. Keynes, *The Economic Consequences of the Peace*, 20.

"functionless investor" or the "rentier."[18] Keynes suggested that the 'euthanasia of the rentier' might be imminent because thrift no longer served a social function. His views became increasingly stringent over time.[19]

Why was Keynes against Savings and future orientation? Keynes' opposition to savings and future orientation has been linked to his personal life. He was a member of the Bloomsbury Group, a collective given over to sexual deviance and rebellion against the customary morals of that era. It was known for its liberal attitudes towards homosexuality. Keynes' biographer, Skidelsky, described the Bloomsbury Group as a "sexual merry-go-around" as members drifted from one partner to another. Further, Keynes and members of this group visited the Mediterranean region multiple times to corrupt little boys.[20] Economist Joseph Schumpeter connected Keynes' "childlessness" and short-run philosophy of life.[21] For this reason, Skidelsky could state that "He [Keynes] was not prepared to risk too much of the present for the sake of a better future . . . ."

There is an integral connection between a man's thinking and his sexual life. Keynes, along with his occasional partner Lytton Strachey, believed that homosexuality represented the pinnacle of existence, surpassing heterosexual relationships.

Contrary to Keynes' belief, the Bible suggests that we do not all perish in the long run. As a parent, I have offspring who will continue to exist beyond my lifespan. When my journey concludes, theirs will persist into the "long run." What values we instill in our children will indeed survive through them. They will impact lives and events beyond one's existence. For this reason, one should defer present gratification.

---

18. A rentier is defined as someone who earns passive income, such as interest from savings, dividends, rents, and so on.

19. Keynes, *The General Theory of Employment, Interest, and Money*, chapter 16, 24.

20. Dobbs, *Keynes at Harvard: Economic Deception as a Political Credo*, 95.

21. Even though Keynes did eventually marry Lydia Lopokova, it was likely just an arrangement as he continued to have male lovers.

In opposition to the Keynesian approach, the Christian perspective, capitalization is seen because of diligent work and thrift, which involves saving. Wealth should not only be accumulated but also spent wisely, as suggested in Hebrews 13:15–16 that we should do good and share with others. The concept of capitalization is closely tied to Christian character. This character is defined by the ability to sacrifice immediate consumption for future benefits, being good stewards of what one has, and acknowledging God in wealth accumulation; a principle found in Deuteronomy 8:17–18, I Corinthians 4:2, Proverbs 21:6, and Proverbs 13:22.[22]

INTELLECTUAL 3: ALFRED CHARLES KINSEY THE SEXOLOGIST

Alfred Kinsey was an American sexologist, biologist, and professor of entomology and zoology. His groundbreaking fraudulent research on human sexuality has had a lasting impact on social and cultural values in the United States and beyond.

Kinsey's fascination with sex stemmed from his scientific curiosity. He sought to understand human sexual behavior. However, was his quest rooted in a desire to find truth and knowledge, or a desire for confession based on personal issues?

As stated earlier, Kinsey's most famous works are "Sexual Behavior in the Human Male" (1948) and "Sexual Behavior in the

---

22. Hebrews 13:15–16 (NIV) Through Jesus, therefore, let us continually offer to God a sacrifice of praise—the fruit of lips that openly profess his name. And do not forget to do good and to share with others, for with such sacrifices God is pleased.

Deuteronomy 8:17–18 (NIV) You may say to yourself, "My power and the strength of my hands have produced this wealth for me." But remember the Lord your God, for it is he who gives you the ability to produce wealth, and so confirms his covenant, which he swore to your ancestors, as it is today.

1 Corinthians 4:2 (NIV) Now it is required that those who have been given a trust must prove faithful.

Proverbs 13:22 (NIV): A good person leaves an inheritance for their children's children,

Proverbs 21:6 (NIV): A fortune made by a lying tongue is a fleeting vapor and a deadly snare.

Human Female" (1953), collectively known as the Kinsey Reports. He collected data through extensive interviews and surveys, covering a wide range of sexual practices and preferences. He skewed this data sample to prisoners, prostitutes, bootleggers, pimps, thieves, etc. He sought his sample from the Chicago underground and prisons and suggested that this was representative of America. Controversially, Kinsey included information about homosexuality, bisexuality, and other "deviant" behaviors. His work also suggested that children were sexual.

Kinsey married Clara McMillen, and they had four children. Their marriage was characterized by openness and experimentation. Kinsey himself identified as both homosexual and a masochist. His personal experiences influenced his research. He discovered homosexual tendencies within himself, which he later suggested were common among a significant portion of the population.[23]

His work paved the way for the sexual revolution of the 1960s. Was his desire to study sex, a thirst for truth, or to self-justify his sexual behaviors? It was the latter and it negatively impacted society.

INTELLECTUAL 4: SIGMUND FREUD THE FOUNDER OF PSYCHOANALYSIS

Sigmund Freud left a mark on psychology and our understanding of the human mind. Freud's groundbreaking work in psychoanalysis revolutionized our understanding of mental processes and behavior. His theories explored the unconscious mind, sexuality, and the dynamics of human relationships. His ideas on civilization, as noted earlier, led Unwin to study various cultures and their rise and fall.

One of Freud's most famous concepts is the Oedipus complex, which he proposed as a universal wish in mankind to commit incest. According to Freud, every child experiences feelings of desire for the opposite-sex parent and rivalry with the same-sex parent.

---

23. Jones, *Degenerate Moderns: Modernity as Rationalized Sexual Misbehavior*, 98, 99.

Born in 1856 in Freiberg, Moravia (now part of the Czech Republic), Freud grew up in a devout Jewish family. He was raised by a nursemaid whom he considered a second mother. Freud's sister-in-law served as a nanny to his children. Some speculate about the nature of their relationship and whether it was sexual, but concrete evidence remains elusive. Freud's own sex life and personal experiences likely influenced his theories, including his exploration of taboo subjects like incest as a form of confession and self-justification.[24]

INTELLECTUAL 5: JOHN MONEY AND TRANSGENDERISM

In the mid-1900s, John Money significantly influenced the fields of human sexual behavior and gender. His work introduced various terminologies such as "gender identity," "sexual orientation," and "gender role." Money believed that gender identity was malleable within the first two years of life. He promoted the idea of surgical "normalization" of the genitalia for intersex infants. His ideas extended to drug treatment for sex offenders to suppress their sex drives. He was also in support of certain aspects of pedophilia.[25]

Money's infamous case involved David Reimer, a twin boy raised as a girl following a botched circumcision. Money advised that David be renamed "Brenda" and raised as a girl. This experiment aimed to prove that gender identity could be shaped through nurture. David and his twin brother, Brian, were coerced into sexual rehearsals with each other, to firmly encode "Brenda's" sexual identity. When the twins refused, they were subject to abuse from Money. These activities were photographed by Money. David's life was troubled, and he eventually "transitioned" back to male. Both David and Brian died by suicide.[26]

---

24. Jones, *Degenerate Moderns: Modernity as Rationalized Sexual Misbehavior*, 139–55.

25. Downing, et al., *Pervert or Sexual Libertarian?: Meet John Money, "the Father of F***Ology,"* paragraph 10, 12.

26. Luke, *John Money, David Reimer, and the Dark Origins of the Transgender*

Money's ideas laid the groundwork for understanding transgenderism. However, the consequences of his work were far-reaching. Parents received misguided advice based on Money's theories. The twins faced verbal abuse during the therapy process. David's transition back to male highlighted the limitations of Money's approach. The experimental procedures used incest and had severe mental health implications.

Did John Money's wild theories come from his libertine lifestyle? He was unbound by societal norms, engaging in both heterosexual and homosexual relationships. His lifestyle included participation in group sex.[27] His personal life influenced his theories, which are deemed as attempts to rationalize his behavior, by conforming truth to desire. As we reckon with the impact of his ideas, we must consider the human cost: lives lost and suffering endured. With the modern transgender movement, infertility-causing surgeries and hormone usage result in shorter time horizons harming economic growth and development.

CONCLUSION

In conclusion, the interplay between sin, guilt, and redemption has fascinated many thinkers. Guilt emerges as a natural consequence of sin—a burden that compels individuals to seek resolution through masochism and sadism. Many also seek self-justification through their works and therefore it is important to know whether intellectuals are living a moral life in their pursuit of truth or whether they are trying to conform truth to desire. People with guilty consciences tend to come to theories and conclusions in ways that align with their immediate desires and short-term thinking hence harming economic growth and prosperity.

Guilt drains social energy and cultural vitality, leading individuals to seek redemption through external mechanisms. The

---

Movement, paragraphs 4, 5, 7, 8.

27. Green, *John Money, Ph.D. (July 8, 1921–July 7, 2006): A Personal Obituary*, 630.

state assumes a redemptive role in response to collective guilt. Citizens, unable to save themselves individually, turn to the state as a savior—a mechanism for creating a redeeming order. However, this results in reduced freedoms, especially economic freedoms. Following God's prescription for sexuality is important for less guilt and is important for liberty in society, which allows for building an expansive civilization. Having repentance and forgiveness through Jesus Christ without delay in one study, allowed Protestants to work harder and more creatively, compared to Catholics and Jews, whose work output became less.[28]

---

28. Henrich suggests that Protestants have "no easy way to wash" one's guilt away compared to Catholics, but I think the explanation is the opposite. Henrich, *The Weirdest People in the World: How the West Became Psychologically Peculiar and Particularly Prosperous*, 423.

9

Afterword

ACCORDING TO UNWIN, IF countries like the U.S. and other historically Christian nations increase in the sexual freedom rankings, there will be an impact on economic freedom and growth. Essentially, sexual freedom and economic freedom are substitutes. Although Unwin did not fully understand the relationship between sexual and economic freedom, the theory of time preferences clarifies why they are substitutes. Societies with low time preferences choose economic freedom, whereas societies that have high time preferences select sexual freedom.

What hope exists for countries like the U.S. and others with a historic Christian heritage, now experiencing a prolonged sexual revolution? Drawing from Adam Smith, J.D. Unwin, and Edward Banfield, the hope lies in having more alpha citizens (or upper-class citizens, as Banfield describes) than beta citizens (or lower-class citizens). Since the sexual revolution in the U.S. was primarily driven by the fraudulent research of Alfred Kinsey, and advocated by the elite voices, the changes to laws are reflective of elite preferences instead of median voter preferences. If there are enough individuals with lower time preferences (alpha citizens) in society, the inevitable decline can be slowed or even reversed as their proportion increases. However, one note of caution, as the Soviets discovered, the sexual revolution can in some societies precipitate rapid decline.

Why did Europe, particularly Northwest Europe, experience sustained economic growth? The Protestant Reformation played a key role by promoting literacy and encouraging Bible reading in native languages. The Reformation instilled new norms in a broader population, which lowered time preferences and extended individuals' time horizons, ultimately benefiting society as a whole. These norms that were absorbed by the population included what Unwin calls "Pauline absolute monogamy," which restricts sexual freedom. Marriage and family became the cornerstone of civilization, with the husband-and-wife relationship symbolizing the bond between Christ and his bride, the Church. Marriage was viewed as a lifelong covenant, with remarriage permitted only under limited circumstances. The family then became enhanced by Christianity, which became "far more than the basic social unit: it was, in essence, the social system"[1] with a present and forward-looking perspective.[2]

Building a low time preference society is a complex task that requires consistent training from a young age, often through Christian education and a deep understanding of the Bible. Without a Christian character that fosters lower time preferences, there is a risk of decapitalization as short-term thinking begins to dominate. Economic systems and conditions such as socialism and inflation are seen as forces that decapitalize society. Therefore, maintaining a Christian character is essential for sustaining capital and ensuring societal progress.

Like Abraham, we need to cultivate a multigenerational perspective, which includes restoring marriage and the family as the center of civilization. This is crucial for leaving a better future for our children. Children raised in two-parent households, with both a father and a mother, tend to fare better in various life outcomes. Conversely, growing up in a single-parent household in a

---

1. Rushdoony, *The Institutes of Biblical Law*, 200.
2. Smith, *Time and Public Policy*, 6, 25.

challenging environment can create compounded challenges for children and society, impacting growth and prosperity.[3]

Although empirical work has started with the coding of the Sexual Freedom Index at the state level, further research across various fields and by different scholars is necessary to explore Unwin's thesis more comprehensively. Additionally, collecting data at the individual level is crucial for empirical analysis to gain deeper insights. This area of research provides scholars with a fertile ground for continued investigation.

---

3. Kearney, *The Two-Parent Privilege: How Americans Stopped Getting Married and Started Falling Behind*, 145, 68–77.

Appendix

From Sexual Freedom to Abortion Access and its Impact on the Future

Brian Baugus & Feler Bose

"Surely these things happened to Judah according to the Lord's command, in order to remove them from his presence because of the sins of Manasseh and all he had done, including the shedding of innocent blood. For he had filled Jerusalem with innocent blood, and the Lord was not willing to forgive."

2 KINGS 24:3–4 (NIV)

ONE OUTCOME OF THE sexual revolution and a lifestyle focused on immediate gratification is the inclination to distance oneself from parental responsibilities. Since raising children involves immediate costs in terms of time and money, individuals with high time preferences are likely to advocate for access to abortion.[1] From an evolutionary viewpoint, the desire to pass on genes is a fundamental drive. However, throughout human history, the acceptance of

---

1. Folbre, *Valuing Children: Rethinking the Economics of the Family*, 15–16.

infanticide, child sacrifice, exposure, and abortion has been the norm, not the exception—a tragic norm that contradicts the evolutionary worldview. Societies that value fetal life and ensure all children are raised until death are the exception rather than the norm.

In many ancient cultures, child sacrifice was indeed practiced for various reasons, such as appeasing deities, ensuring good harvests, or possibly joining elite clubs.[2] However, cultural practices, including those involving child sacrifice, have varied widely across different societies and historical periods. The advent of Christianity brought significant changes to these practices. Christian teachings emphasized the sanctity of life, which contributed to the decline of child sacrifice, exposure, infanticide, and abortion in regions where Christianity spread.

Other major world religions such as Buddhism, Zoroastrianism, Hinduism, Islam, and Judaism, as well as ancient codes such as the Code of Hammurabi condemn abortion. Exceptions are made for saving the life of the mother.[3] However, the actual practice on the ground may have been different.

Even within Christianity, it's important to note that while Christians were committed to anti-infanticide and anti-abortion positions, the biographies of Christian elites often show suspiciously few siblings and children which could be due to disease, maintaining social standing, and inheritance issues.[4] Among elite Christian households, abortion, and infanticide continued well into the 5th or 6th centuries due to the privacy that was afforded them by their wealth.[5] Further, the top-down conversion at the time of Emperor Constantine likely meant that many elites'

---

2. Bose, *Does the New World Order Worship Satan? Using Rational Choice to Understand Qanon*, 154.

3. Whittler, *Abortions in World Religions*, 1–5.

4. Bakke, *When Children Became People: The Birth of Childhood in Early Christianity*, 138.

5. Betancourt, *Abortion and Contraception in the Middle Ages: Both Were Far More Common Than You Might Think*, 12th paragraph.

conversions to Christianity were politically expedient and not a matter of confession.[6]

With the advent of sustained economic growth, which allowed societies to escape subsistence living as envisioned by Malthus, the economic argument for infanticide was significantly weakened, enabling anti-infanticidal norms to spread more broadly. The spread of Christianity provided a moral framework to reinforce these norms, but perhaps, the spread of "anti-infanticidal economic structures did as much to spread these religions as the religions did to spread anti-infanticide norms."[7]

Children help extend individuals' time horizons to the next generation and hence children are important. Practices such as child sacrifice, exposure, infanticide, and abortion can foster a high-time preference society, even when these actions are taken to supposedly ensure the survival and prosperity of the larger family or community. Therefore, we theorize that a culture promoting such practices is characterized by high time preferences, negatively impacting development. Additionally, as mentioned in Chapter 8, dealing with guilt from murdering one's child, can further hinder economic development.

In the next section, we will explore the history of abortion in the U.S., highlighting the challenges in eliminating the practice and how progress made over certain decades can be undone in subsequent ones. Additionally, in this chapter we will review the literature on abortion, examining whether a woman obtaining an abortion benefits her in the short term and in the long term.

U.S. ABORTION HISTORY IN BRIEF

As Christian doctrine spread and was internalized by individuals and families, it shifted society from that of high time preference to low time preference i.e., to longer time horizons. Consistent with the internalization of these norms, Christians have worked hard

---

6. Stark and Finke, *Acts of Faith: Explaining the Human Side of Religion*, 69.

7. https://x.com/lymanstoneky/status/1543205225187647489 (accessed September 4, 2024).

over the generations to save those vulnerable including unborn children. Throughout history and across the world, those who hold ideas about the dignity of humans, including unborn humans, have been a vocal minority trying to inhibit the "utilitarian majority" from killing their offspring born and unborn.

The U.S. has also struggled to contain abortion even though it has strong Christian roots. Generally, when social problems arose during the 18th and 19th centuries, churches, families, and private groups were called upon to provide a solution. Only when private efforts failed did the state get involved legislatively.[8]

In 1710, the Virginia colony passed an Act entitled "An Act to prevent the destroying and murdering of Bastard Children" In an attempt to prevent women from concealing pregnancies and then killing newborn illegitimate children. It carried the death penalty. Other colonies followed suit but with varying penalties.[9] In 1801, Kentucky adopted the Virginia law with a less severe punishment of two to seven years imprisonment. Georgia passed a similar law in 1816, with penalties of up to one year in prison, more if murder could be proven. With the increase in prostitution in the 1830s, other states and federal territories also passed anti-concealment laws.[10]

As the preferred method for ending a life moved from infanticide (with or without concealing) to abortion, the laws started adopting to reflect the change. In 1821, Connecticut passed a "crimes and punishments" law that included a section against abortion, the first of its kind.

In the 1830s, newspaper circulation grew, sustained by revenue from advertising, including that for abortions, which featured such euphemisms as curing "irregularity of females." Legislatures during this period had to deal with how to contain abortion when there were no corpses, no autopsies, few if any witnesses,

---

8. Olasky, *Abortion Rites: A Social History of Abortion in America*, 85.

9. The difficulty in convincing the jury beyond a reasonable doubt that the mother killed her baby was the reason many colonies/states moved away from the death penalty for the mother.

10. Olasky, *Abortion Rites: A Social History of Abortion in America*, 86ff.

second-hand declarations, dying declarations, etc. Some of the abortifacients even had beneficial uses. How could a prosecutor convince a jury that a crime even occurred? The New York Legislature found itself enacting and amending laws concerning abortion ten times from 1828 to 1881.[11] Some states had insignificant penalties for women to encourage them to testify that an abortion had occurred. Other states gave the woman immunity for her testimony if she had an abortion. This generated the evidence prosecutors needed to pursue abortionists in court.[12]

Between 1840 and 1860, states had passed many anti-advertising laws against abortion. Only thirteen of the thirty-three states had yet to pass any antiabortion laws. At least thirteen states had laws banning abortions during all stages of pregnancy and other states still had the quickening distinctive.[13],[14]

More antiabortion laws went into effect between 1860 and 1880, and punishment was meted out to those who tried to induce abortions before quickening. If the jury was convinced that an abortion occurred, then the punishment was to be more severe. Some states defined abortion as "manslaughter." Some imposed the same penalty for both deaths if the mother and the unborn child died during an abortion. Some states, to increase prosecution of abortion-related cases, removed the requirement that pregnancy be proved. After the Civil War, many southern states passed antiabortion laws, which stood even after the northern troops left.[15] Mohr writing about this time says that the "fundamental legal doctrines [the laws] embodied were destined to remain little changed for a hundred years."[16]

---

11. Olasky, *Abortion Rites: A Social History of Abortion in America*, 96.

12. Olasky, *Abortion Rites: A Social History of Abortion in America*, 99.

13. Mohr, *Abortion in America: The Origins and Evolution of National Policy*, 1800–1900, 145.

14. Olasky, *Abortion Rites: A Social History of Abortion in America*, 102.

15. Olasky, *Abortion Rites: A Social History of Abortion in America*, 102.

16. Mohr, *Abortion in America: The Origins and Evolution of National Policy*, 1800–1900, 201.

APPENDIX

Between 1880 and 1900, abortion was illegal in the United States. The various states' laws were now unambiguous in their condemnation of abortion. Furthermore, the courts took a harder stance against abortion.

At the beginning of the 20th century, various state laws prohibited abortions, and the Comstock Law banned the transmission via the federal postal system of "obscene and lascivious" material, which included birth control material. However, by 1973, abortion was legalized in all 50 states for any reason.

A history of abortion in the 20th century would be incomplete without a discussion of Margaret Sanger. In 1942, she founded "Planned Parenthood" to convey a wholesome image; then brought numerous other birth control organizations under the Planned Parenthood umbrella and followed with a massive advertising blitz that, while she hid her radical leanings and illicit affairs, focused on "patriotism and family values."[17]

After World War II, pro-abortion strategists built on their 1930s gradualism, hoping to sway the median voter with public relations campaigns suggesting that anti-abortion laws violated the separation of church and state, that anti-abortion laws hurt women, that the only way to stop illegal abortion was to legalize it and that legalization would prevent maternal death.[18]

Pro-abortionists advocated legal abortions for rape victims and certain hardship cases in addition to cases involving the health of the mother. Newspapers openly advocated abortion without conveying the whole truth, to shift the median voter preferences to support the liberalizing of abortion laws. Newspapers started reporting the number of illegal abortions as high as 1,300,000 without substantiation. And left the impression that most abortions were done under non-sterile conditions. The pro-abortion Kinsey Institute estimated that at least 85% of abortions were in sterile environments.[19]

---

17. Grant, *Grand Illusions: The Legacy of Planned Parenthood*, 62.
18. Olasky, *The Press and Abortion 1938–1988*, 78.
19. Olasky, *The Press and Abortion 1938–1988*, 88–90.

APPENDIX

The print media advocated more flexibility in abortion law[20] and started writing more favorably about abortion but very little was said about the unborn child; instead, the discussion pitted "good abortionists" against "butcher quacks" and focused on the risks to the mother.[21]

From the 1960s, the movement to legalize abortion proceeded rapidly. Two key focusing events proved to be boons to those marketing abortion to the median voter via the media. When birth defects resulting from thalidomide use during pregnancy prompted one Arizona woman, who was unable to get an abortion here, to travel abroad to get one, the media gave overwhelming national coverage to her plight and argued that the law preventing her abortion was cruel. The second event was the epidemic of German measles in 1964, a disease that could cause birth defects. These two events led to increased legislative support of the American Law Institute's (ALI) legal code which advocated for legalized abortion for cases involving rape, incest, fetal deformity, and if the doctor believed that continuing the pregnancy was a risk to the mother's physical or mental health.[22],[23] In 1967, Colorado adopted the ALI model code. By 1972, thirteen states had ALI-type statutes in the books while thirty-one states allowed abortion only to save the mother's life.

Success in legalizing abortion through legislative means was further limited; so pro-abortion forces focused their attention on the courts. The pro-abortion interest groups were able to maximize the ideological interests of judges more effectively than those of legislators.[24] Building on precedent, these interest groups were able to move the Courts in their direction as shown by *Griswold v. Connecticut* (1965) in which the Supreme Court

20. Sauer, *Attitudes to Abortion in America, 1800–1973*, 63.

21. Olasky, *The Press and Abortion 1938–1988*, 88ff.

22. Olasky, *The Press and Abortion 1938–1988*, 91.

23. Blanchard, *The Anti-Abortion Movement and the Rise of the Religious Right: From Polite to Fiery Protest*, 22.

24. Pritchard and Zywicki, *Finding the Constitution: An Economic Analysis of Tradition's Role in Constitutional Interpretation*, 494.

found the right to marital privacy in the issues of contraception. The Supreme Court extended the right to privacy to unmarried couples in *Eisenstadt v. Baird* (1972). Finally, in 1973, in *Roe v. Wade* (1973), the Supreme Court said that the right to privacy includes abortion and, further, in *Doe v. Bolton* (1973), defined "health of a woman" in terms so broad that abortion was legalized for any reason. These rulings were beyond what the median voter preferences indicated at that time.[25]

ARE THERE SHORT-TERM OR LONG-TERM BENEFITS FROM GETTING ABORTIONS?

Since Roe v. Wade legalized abortions for any reason, health considerations ceased to be the primary factor. Women often seek abortions due to the financial burden of having a baby, a reason supported by numerous studies. Financial instability is a significant factor influencing their decision, even when they have doubts or a desire to continue the pregnancy. Abortion is seen as a low-cost solution compared to the high costs of unexpected pregnancies, which can preserve educational and employment prospects and promote economic growth and prosperity.

Some research shows that access to abortion has allowed women, particularly Black women, to pursue further education and increase workforce participation.[26] However, many of these studies are suggestive rather than conclusive, often focusing on short-term impacts due to data limitations. Data collection, analysis, and reliability issues, such as reliance on self-reported data, also affect these findings.

Despite these challenges, some research indicates that abortion legalization has positively impacted women's wages and

---

25. A paper by Blake surveys a number of polls around 1973 that indicates that a majority did not desire unrestricted abortion. Blake, *The Supreme Court's Abortion Decisions and Public Opinion in the United States*, 51–60.

26. Bernstein and Jones, *The Economic Effects of Abortion Access: A Review of the Evidence*, v.

APPENDIX

educational attainment. However, the long-term economic benefits remain a topic of debate and largely unexplored.

Numerous studies also challenge or at least raise serious concerns about the robustness of these conclusions. Many of the papers that conclude that abortion is a net positive financial outcome for women tend to be short-term in nature and rather narrowly focused. Table A-1 summarizes some of the most important studies that raise significant concerns about the dominant conclusions but one in particular captures the problems and biases of many of the studies in the field and demonstrates that long-term implications may not be as advertised.

In 2016, Mølland published a paper examining the impact of abortion availability on young women and their children through a natural experiment in Norway. This type of experiment is highly sought after by social science researchers. Between 1969 and 1972, Oslo liberalized abortion access, while the rest of Norway maintained stricter regulations.

In the late 1960s, Norwegian women could apply for an abortion for limited reasons, with their husband's consent if married. The application was reviewed by a two-doctor panel, often requiring the woman to defend her case in person. Although abortion was legalized in Norway in 1964, access was very limited before 1969. For instance, in 1968, the abortion rate was 8 per 1,000 unmarried women in Oslo and even lower elsewhere in Norway.

From 1969 to 1972, Oslo's liberalized approach led to a significant increase in abortion rates, reaching about 27 per 1,000 unmarried women in 1972 and over 30 per 1,000 in 1975. In contrast, the rest of Norway, with a stricter interpretation of the law, did not see rates exceed 10 per 1,000 until 1972.[27]

Mølland highlights that, in addition to the more liberal legal approach in Oslo, the uniform laws were interpreted and enforced differently there. The medical culture in Oslo was more inclined to approve abortion applications, and the city had more doctors and free clinics to assist women with the process.

27. Mølland, *Benefits from Delay? The Effect of Abortion Availability on Young Women and Their Children*, 8.

APPENDIX

This situation enabled Mølland to investigate the employment and economic effects on women who were otherwise identical, except for their access to abortion. He discovered a small but notable short-term positive impact on earnings from abortion, but a significant negative impact in the long run. Many studies in the literature highlight the short-term benefits of abortion, but Mølland reveals the bias in these studies and cautions against drawing broad conclusions from such limited and short-term analyses.

But his findings even challenge some short-run conclusions; "[U]sing the rest of Norway as the control group... I do not find any effect on the likelihood of finishing high school or on years of education, but I do find a positive effect on obtaining a college degree that is about 1.8% and statistically significant...and I conclude that abortion access led to increases in educational investments for these women."[28] So, his results suggest that abortion access does not improve high school graduation rates but of those who did graduate, they were a little more likely to go to college. So, this must carry over into the labor market and employment and wage outcomes, and it does for a little while.

MØlland reports that abortion access led to higher full-time employment but only "until about age 35 with the magnitude being about 3% in the late 20s and early 30s." However, women who had an abortion "are *less* likely to be employed full-time in their late 30s and during their 40s with the size of the effect being about 2 or 3%" but "[T]he effect sizes get smaller as women get towards their 50s but remain... statistically significant." Women who had abortion access have higher earnings in their mid-20s but have lower earnings subsequently. The earnings differences are rarely statistically significant until women reach between about 35 and 45 at which point there is a significant negative effect (from abortion) of about 5%. After age 45, the earnings penalty to early abortion access gets smaller and generally becomes statistically insignificant."[29] Access to abortion seems to give women a quick

28. Mølland, *Benefits from Delay? The Effect of Abortion Availability on Young Women and Their Children*, 12.

29. Mølland, *Benefits from Delay? The Effect of Abortion Availability on*

head-start in the labor market but it is unsustainable and women without access to abortion catch and pass the women with access in the long run.

It might be reasonable to conclude from MØlland's work that women who gave birth while young, were delayed in their careers, and once they entered or re-entered the workforce, it took some time, but eventually, they caught up. And, when those women who had aborted while young and delayed childbearing and had a career interruption as they entered motherhood in their late 20s through mid-30s they lost their lead and early career gains. Once child-rearing was over for both groups, there was income convergence regardless of their abortion decisions. That story seems logical and consistent and is completely wrong as MØlland explains that women with early access to abortion had a noticeable increase in the probability that they would *never* have children. However, for many women, abortion access allowed for women to postpone fertility.[30] Some of these women never became mothers, which suggests that while the above explanation may be true in some cases, other significant factors are at work in reducing the demand for children and impacting economic outcomes.

There is much more to MØlland's research than can be adequately surmised in a short chapter, and to be fair, he does find some positives to early abortion access. But his findings that much of the benefit, especially in employment, is not long-lasting is an important aspect that many do not acknowledge or possibly even know. The articles in the table below (Table A-1) also offer some important critiques of the prevailing narrative that abortions are a net positive for women.

Young Women and Their Children, 12,13.

30. Mølland, *Benefits from Delay? The Effect of Abortion Availability on Young Women and Their Children*, 12.

Table A-1: Summary of Selected Studies of the Economics and Employment Impact of Abortion.

Author	Year	Nature of Study	Relevant Conclusions
Zabin, et. al.[31]	1989	A 2-year study of 360 black unmarried girls under 17 years of age who had a pregnancy test regardless of outcome. Girls were interviewed at 6-month intervals	Girls who obtained an abortion were better off, even after 2 years (pp. 250–1) But the measure was of household income not of the girls themselves and is an example of how many of these studies do not measure what is relevant (p. 250). Girls who got subsequent abortions lost whatever benefits the first one gave them and did not have better outcomes on any measure (pp. 252–3)
Fergusson *et. al.*[32]	2007	A 25-year longitudinal study of life outcomes of 492 New Zealand women, 125 of which had at least one pregnancy by age 21	Found that women who underwent abortion were more likely to earn a university degree (p. 7) But those women came from households where that was true regardless of pregnancy status (p. 8) Women who aborted despite a college degree showed no differences in any of economic outcome (p. 10)

31. Zabin, et al., *When Urban Adolescents Choose Abortion: Effects on Education, Psychological Status and Subsequent Pregnancy*, 250–53.

32. Fergusson, et al., *Abortion among Young Women and Subsequent Life Outcomes*, 7,9,10.

APPENDIX

Mølland[33]	2016	Studied the impact on Norwegian women after Oslo relaxed restrictions on abortion while the rest of Norway did not	Abortion access led to higher full-time employment "until about age 35" (p. 12) However, women who had an abortion "are *less* likely to be employed full-time in their late 30s and during their 40s" (p. 12) A difference that shrinks some but remains statistically significant into their 50's (p. 13) Women who had abortion access have higher earnings in their mid-20s but have lower earnings subsequently. (p. 13) After age 35 there is a significant negative effect on earnings from abortion which begins to shrink after age 45 compared to women who did not abort (p. 13)
Steingrimsdottir[34]	2016	Study of 18-year old women with early legal access to abortion	Such access changes career plans to careers associated with a 1–2% lower income and lower prestige jobs compared to their peer group in the general population (p. 36) Impact mainly affects women in the low ability group (p. 36) Men benefit significantly when women have early legal access to abortion (p. 36) Access to abortion is associated with higher prestige scores among high ability men. (p. 36)

33. Mølland, *Benefits from Delay? The Effect of Abortion Availability on Young Women and Their Children*, 12,13.

34. Steingrimsdottir, *Reproductive Rights and the Career Plans of U.S. College Freshmen*, 36.

Everett, et. al.[35]	2019	A follow-up on Steingrimsdottir	Males are the primary beneficiaries of legal and easy access to abortion (p. 520) "[M]en benefit from the physical and emotional labor of women who elect to terminate adolescent pregnancies...For each of these pregnancies, there is a male partner who either knowingly or not may be positively impacted by a woman's decision to have an abortion." (p. 525).

From the articles above and their findings, it is a reasonable conclusion that for women undergoing abortion, there are potentially some advantages but also some disadvantages, but they are not evenly or randomly distributed. Women coming from higher-income and stable families tend to do well financially after an abortion. The evidence suggests that economically they continue at the same level, if they do not undergo a second abortion. There is no evidence, however, to support the contention that these women attain success *because* of abortion. Women coming from less wealthy and less stable families seem to do even worse post-abortion. However, it seems that no matter the circumstances, the primary beneficiaries from a woman's "right to choose" are men, who are no longer attached to a woman and child they may have had no long-term interest in, and who are free to move on with their lives with minimal disruption.

In addition to the questions about the scope and focus and therefore the robustness of the conclusions of the studies showing financial advantages from abortion, there is also a question about the nature and methodology of these studies. One popular and frequently referenced study is called the Turnaway Study. The Atlantic magazine called it "The most important study in the abortion debate."[36] This study compares women who got an abortion with

---

35. Everett, et al., *Male Abortion Beneficiaries: Exploring the Long-Term Educational and Economic Associations of Abortion among Men Who Report Teen Pregnancy*, 520, 25.

36. Lowrey, *The Most Important Study in the Abortion Debate*, title.

those who were turned away due to being past the gestational limit. This study finds many benefits for women who receive abortions (mental health benefits, physical health benefits, positive socio-economic impacts, and overall well-being) versus those who were turned away. One of the main issues is that many of these positive conclusions contradict studies done in other countries. Further, the researchers do not make their data available for replication and review. There are numerous research and review issues including:

- investigators do not clearly articulate the sampling plan,
- the size of the population, or
- precisely how sites situated in different cities were chosen, and
- the cities are not identified.

The researchers only provide general information on these issues, making it impossible to replicate the study or test it meaningfully. A study that is considered the gold standard by many and frequently referenced by other researchers should be transparent and above reproach from a methodological point of view but as one critic put it "[W]idespread dissemination of misinformation generated from studies like the Turnaway Study, hundreds of thousands of women considering an abortion are likely unaware of the expansive literature demonstrating abortion is a significant risk factor for post-abortion psychological distress and mental health detriments."[37]

Studies done in other countries contradict the Turnaway Study conclusions. A Danish study using large-scale population data found that, compared to women who had only given birth, mortality rates were higher for women who had undergone an induced abortion (470%), induced abortion and natural loss (340%), induced abortion, natural loss, and birth (20.9%), and induced abortion and birth (30%). This suggests that even choosing to have a child after an abortion increases the mortality rate.

37. Coleman, *The Turnaway Study: A Case of Self-Correction in Science Upended by Political Motivation and Unvetted Findings*, 9.

APPENDIX

Additionally, in a controlled model, women who had an induced abortion (66%) and those in the induced abortion and birth group (56%) had a higher risk of death compared to the only birth group. Furthermore, having multiple abortions increased mortality risk, whereas multiple births reduced it.[38]

One study finds that substance use disorder is prevalent in women having had one abortion.[39] A Danish study found that women with "a recent induced abortion still have a 2-fold suicide risk" and suggested further investigation.[40] A Korean study found that women who had three or more abortions had higher levels of suicidal ideation.[41] For these reasons, mental health concerns should not be ignored.

Making abortion more accessible also increases the incidence of sexually transmitted disease (STDs like gonorrhea and syphilis) as abortion accessibility increases risky sexual activity.[42] These STDs will need short-term and ongoing treatment, bringing about economic loss.

Increased sexual activity out of wedlock due to a lower risk of giving birth has other consequences. Sexual risk taking occurs with individuals who have higher discount rates, and they regret their choices later.[43]

Further, according to CDC data, most abortions are of those who are unmarried. About 86 percent nationally in 2020.[44] This is

38. Coleman, et al., *Reproductive History Patterns and Long-Term Mortality Rates: A Danish, Population-Based Record Linkage Study*, 570.

39. Mota, et al., *Associations between Abortion, Mental Disorders, and Suicidal Behaviour in a Nationally Representative Sample*, 240.

40. Gissler, et al., *Decreased Suicide Rate after Induced Abortion, after the Current Care Guidelines in Finland 1987–2012*,

41. Wie, et al., *The Association between Abortion Experience and Postmenopausal Suicidal Ideation and Mental Health: Results from the 5th Korean National Health and Nutrition Examination Survey (Knhanes V)*,

42. Klick and Stratmann, *The Effect of Abortion Legalization on Sexual Behavior: Evidence from Sexually Transmitted Diseases*, 407.

43. Chesson, et al., *Discount Rates and Risky Sexual Behaviors among Teenagers and Young Adults*, 217.

44. Abortion Surveillance — United States, 2020 | MMWR (cdc.gov)

APPENDIX

due to unstable relationships of the unmarried and the higher time preferences of the nature of the relationships. Restricting abortion will incentivize people to choose better long-term partners that could result in marriage which then improves the welfare of children. "Children of married parents are physically and mentally healthier, better educated, and later in life, enjoy more career success than children in other family settings."[45] Better choices in marriage impact society positively as it promotes longer time horizons, resulting in economic growth and prosperity.

CONCLUSION

Some research concludes, and many proponents of abortion claim, that abortion improves economic outcomes for women. On its surface, the suggestion that killing human babies (or whatever term they care to use, it is still a human life) is a positive thing to do is maybe the ultimate act of self-centeredness. At its core abortion is the act of killing a completely defenseless life for the convenience of the killer, who happens to be the one person who is supposed to protect that very life. Of course, there are exceptions, but exceptions do not make the rule. The absurd, demented logic that somehow some adults will be better off if some babies are not allowed to exist shows how low many people hold human value and dignity and how poorly we understand economics and even basic biology. It assumes that a new person is merely a mouth to feed, a drain on a fixed amount of resources, and that in a struggle to capture more resources for oneself even the killing of one's offspring is acceptable. But this is where we are, engaging in the scholarly and political debate over an action that seems so self-damaging and barbaric that we call people who used to engage in this behavior pagans, idol worshippers, and savages.

The moral vacuity of this action is why a closer examination of the research shows these claims of a positive financial aspect to

---

(accessed January 28, 2023).

45. Waite and Gallagher, *The Case for Marriage: Why Married People Are Happier, Healthier, and Better Off Financially*, 124.

abortion have questionable support. Abortion, birth, and family planning are complex and highly emotional issues that are difficult to study. All claims should be made with caution, recognizing that any conclusions are associated with many caveats. As Coast et al. stated in their review of abortion's microeconomic costs, "[V]ery little evidence [in the literature] specifically uses the language of the economic benefits and values of abortion; much of the evidence included here is based on interpretation of relevant evidence." They conclude that "Many gaps remain in our evidence base around the microeconomic impacts of abortion, including the indirect economic impact of abortion-related care and the longer-term economic impacts."[46]

The evidence that abortion improves education outcomes for women is thin, and there is almost no evidence it improves long-term economic outcomes. Many women, after having abortions fail to have children later thereby limiting the time horizons of the family unit.[47] Executing capital punishment on the fetus does not benefit society. The revulsion for life is a mark of a declining culture and a desire to assume control over life and death by playing god. And as 2 Kings 24:3–4 states, at some point, the shedding of innocent blood results in no more forgiveness being available from the Lord for the land resulting in a "determined and irreversible judgment" resulting in economic devastation.[48]

It seems that men who impregnate women out of wedlock can capture significant income and career benefits if the woman undergoes an abortion. Interestingly this seems to be at least tacitly acknowledged from the beginning. At a 1989 National Abortion Rights Action League (NARAL) conference, feminist icon Betty Friedan was the guest speaker asked to reflect on the feminist movement and abortion in particular. In her talk, she discusses

46. Coast, et al., *The Microeconomics of Abortion: A Scoping Review and Analysis of the Economic Consequences for Abortion Care-Seekers*, 12, 13.

47. Mølland, *Benefits from Delay? The Effect of Abortion Availability on Young Women and Their Children*, 12.

48. Blackburn, *The Destroyer of Peace: On Abortion as a Matter of National Welfare*, 17.

APPENDIX

how it was mostly men who helped organize and form NARAL and push for legal abortion and specifically referred to writer and activist Larry Lader as the godfather of both the feminist movement and the abortion rights movement.[49]

Christians continue to lobby against abortion in many countries as they have in the past. In the U.S., this has resulted in the *Dobbs v. Jackson Women's Health Organization*, 597 U.S. 215 (2022) decision. It has shifted the decision of abortion to the states where the battle for unborn children, and the future, continues to rage.

---

49. C-Span, *Who Decides? Political Action for Pro-Choice: Betty Friedan_Men Influenced Abortion.*

Bibliography

Acemoglu, Daron, Simon Johnson, and James A. Robinson. "The Colonial Origins of Comparative Development: An Empirical Investigation." *The American Economic Review* 91, no. 5 (2001): 1369–401. http://www.jstor.org/stable/2677930.

"AIDS and IV Drug Use." In *Aids, Sexual Behavior, and Intravenous Drug Use*, edited by Charles F. Turner, Heather G. Miller and Lincoln E. Moses. Washington, D.C.: National Academies 1989.

Aksoy, Cevat G., Christopher S. Carpenter, Ralph De Haas, and Kevin D. Tran. "Do Laws Shape Attitudes? Evidence from Same-Sex Relationship Recognition Policies in Europe." *European Economic Review* 124 (2020): 1–18. https://doi.org/10.1016/j.euroecorev.2020.103399.

Allyn, David. "Private Acts/Public Policy: Alfred Kinsey, the American Law Institute and the Privatization of American Sexual Morality." *Journal of American Studies* 30, no. 3 (1996): 405–28. http://www.jstor.org/stable/27556177.

Ardrey, Robert. *African Genesis: A Personal Investigation in the Animal Origins and Nature of Man.* New York: Dell Publishing Co., Inc., 1961.

Arruñada, Benito. "Protestants and Catholics: Similar Work Ethic, Different Social Ethic." *The Economic Journal* 120, no. 547 (2010): 890–918. https://doi.org/10.1111/j.1468-0297.2009.02325.x.

Baker, Leonard. *Brandeis and Frankfurter : A Dual Biography.* New York: Harper & Row, 1984.

Bakke, Odd M. *When Children Became People: The Birth of Childhood in Early Christianity.* Translated by Brian McNeill. Minneapolis, MN: Fortress, 2005.

Banfield, Edward C. *The Unheavenly City: The Nature and Future of Our Urban Crisis.* Boston: Little, Brown and Company, 1970.

Bauer, Peter T. *Dissent on Development: Studies and Debates in Development Economics.* Cambridge, MA: Harvard University Press, 1976.

Becker, Gary S., and Casey B. Mulligan. "The Endogenous Determination of Time Preference." *The Quarterly Journal of Economics* 112, no. 3 (1997): 729–58. http://www.jstor.org/stable/2951254.

BIBLIOGRAPHY

Belsky, Jay, Avshalom Caspi, Terrie E. Moffitt, and Richie Poulton. *The Origins of You: How Childhood Shapes Later Life*. Cambridge: Harvard University Press, 2020.

Bernstein, Anna, and Kelly M. Jones. *The Economic Effects of Abortion Access: A Review of the Evidence*. Institute for Women's Policy Research (2019). http://www.jstor.org/stable/resrep34541.

Betancourt, Roland. "Abortion and Contraception in the Middle Ages: Both Were Far More Common Than You Might Think." *Scientific American Health & Medicine* 3, no. 1 (2021).

Blackburn, W. Ross. "The Destroyer of Peace: On Abortion as a Matter of National Welfare." *Touchstone: A Journal of Mere Christianity* January/February (2013): 17–18.

Blake, Judith. "The Supreme Court's Abortion Decisions and Public Opinion in the United States." *Population and Development Review* 3, no. 1/2 (1977): 45–62.

Blanchard, Dallas A. *The Anti-Abortion Movement and the Rise of the Religious Right: From Polite to Fiery Protest*. New York: Twayne Publishers, 1994.

Boerner, Lars, and Battista Severgnini. *Time for Growth*. King's College (London: 2019).

Bolt, Jutta, and Jan Luiten van Zanden. "Maddison-Style Estimates of the Evolution of the World Economy: A New 2023 Update." *Journal of Economic Surveys* (2023): 1–41. https://doi.org/10.1111/joes.12618.

Bose, Feler. "A Contractual Look at the Role of Religion in the Stability of Marriage." *Journal of Economics, Theology and Religion* 1, no. 1 (2021): 45–63.

———. "The Determinants of Sexual Freedom from 1990 to 2010." *Applied Economics Letters* 22, no. 15 (2015): 1224–29. https://doi.org/10.1080/13504851.2015.1021449.

———. "Does the New World Order Worship Satan? Using Rational Choice to Understand Qanon." *Journal for the Study of Radicalism* 18, no. 1 (2024): 147–78. https://doi.org/10.14321/jstudradi.18.1.0147.

———. "Law Order Vs. Lawyer Order: Analyzing the Development of Jury Independence." *Journal of Libertarian Studies* 24, no. 2 (2020): 272–92.

———. *License to Sin: The Politics and Opportunity Cost of Sexual Freedom*. 2013. Available at SSRN: http://dx.doi.org/10.2139/ssrn.2039060

———. "Policy Innovativeness and Sexual Freedom." *Social Science Quarterly* 102, no. 4 (2021): 1496–510. https://doi.org/10.1111/ssqu.12984.

Bose, Feler, and Jeffry A Jacob. "Changing Sexual Regulations in the U.S. From 1990 to 2010: Spatial Panel Data Analysis." *Review of Economics and Institutions* 9, no. 1 (2018): 1–18. https://doi.org/10.5202/rei.v9i1.21418.

Bose, Feler, and Zachary Van Duyn. "Time Preferences as Partisan Politics: What Do Party Manifestos Show in Twenty-Two Oecd Countries?." *European Politics and Society* (2020): 1–16. https://doi.org/10.1080/23745118.2020.1847571.

BIBLIOGRAPHY

Boudreaux, Donald J. "Donald J. Boudreaux, "Deirdre Mccloskey and Economists' Ideas About Ideas." *Liberty Matters*, 2014.

Breyer, Stephen. "The Interdependence of Science and Law." *Science*, 1998, 537–38.

Buth, Lenore. *How to Talk Confidently to Your Child About Sex*. St. Louis, MO: Concordia 1998.

Who Decides? Political Action for Pro-Choice: Betty Friedan_Men Influenced Abortion,1989, on C-Span. https://www.c-span.org/video/?c4744103/user-clip-betty-friedan-men-influenced-abortion.

Calderone, Mary S. *Siecus Report*. Sex Information and Education Council of the U.S. (New York: 1982).

Calhoun, John B. "Population Density and Social Pathology." *Scientific American* 206, no. 2 (1962): 139–48.

Cameron, Paul. *Sexual Gradualism: A Solution to the Sexual Dilemma of Teen-Agers and Young Adults*. Sun Valley, CA: HumLife, 1978.

Chesson, Harrell W., Jami S. Leichliter, Gregory D. Zimet, Susan L. Rosenthal, David I. Bernstein, and Kenneth H. Fife. "Discount Rates and Risky Sexual Behaviors among Teenagers and Young Adults." *Journal of Risk and Uncertainty* 32, no. 3 (2006): 217–30. https://doi.org/10.1007/s11166-006-9520-1.

Chilton, David. *Productive Christians in an Age of Guilt-Manipulators: A Biblical Response to Ronald J. Sider*. Tyler, TX: Institute for Christian Economics, 1981.

Chubb, John. *The Fate of Empires and Search for Survival*. Edinburgh, Scotland: William Blackwood & Sons Ltd, 1977.

Clarkson, Joshua J., John R. Chambers, Edward R. Hirt, Ashley S. Otto, Frank R. Kardes, and Christopher Leone. "The Self-Control Consequences of Political Ideology." *Proceedings of the National Academy of Sciences* 112, no. 27 (2015): 8250–53. https://doi.org/10.1073/pnas.1503530112.

Coast, E., S. R. Lattof, Y. V. Meulen Rodgers, B. Moore, and C. Poss. "The Microeconomics of Abortion: A Scoping Review and Analysis of the Economic Consequences for Abortion Care-Seekers." *PLoS One* 16, no. 6 (2021): 1–21. https://doi.org/10.1371/journal.pone.0252005.

Cochran, William G., Frederick Mosteller, and John W. Tukey. "Statistical Problems of the Kinsey Report." *Journal of the American Statistical Association* 48, no. 264 (1953): 673–716. https://doi.org/10.2307/2281066.

Coleman, Phyllis. "Who's Been Sleeping in My Bed? You and Me, and the State Makes Three." *Indiana Law Review* 24, no. 2 (1991): 399–416.

Coleman, Priscilla K. "The Turnaway Study: A Case of Self-Correction in Science Upended by Political Motivation and Unvetted Findings." *Frontiers in Psychology* 13 (2022): 1–11.

Coleman, Priscilla K., David C. Reardon, and Byron C. Calhoun. "Reproductive History Patterns and Long-Term Mortality Rates: A Danish, Population-Based Record Linkage Study." *European Journal of Public Health* 23, no. 4 (2012): 569–74. https://doi.org/10.1093/eurpub/cks107.

BIBLIOGRAPHY

Cooter, Robert D. "The Rule of State Law and the Rule-of-Law State: Economic Analysis of the Legal Foundations of Development." *The International Bank for Reconstruction and Development/The World Bank* (1997): 191–217.

Diamond, Jared. *Guns Germs and Steel: The Fates of Human Societies.* New York: W.W. Norton, 1997.

Dobbs, Zygmund. *Keynes at Harvard: Economic Deception as a Political Credo.* West Sayville, NY: Veritas Study, 1969 (2009).

Downing, Lisa, Iain Morland, and Nikki Sullivan. "Pervert or Sexual Libertarian?: Meet John Money, "the Father of F***Ology."" *Salon*, 2015.

Egan, Seán. "The Bolsheviks and the Sexual Revolution." *Irish Marxist Review* 6 (2017): 36–41.

Elias, Norbert. *The Civilizing Process: The History of Manners.* Translated by Edmund Jephcott. 2 vols. Vol. 1, New York: Pantheon Books, 1978.

Ensminger, Jean. "Transaction Costs and Islam: Explaining Conversion in Africa." *Journal of Institutional and Theoretical Economics (JITE) / Zeitschrift für die gesamte Staatswissenschaft* 153, no. 1 (1997): 4–29. http://www.jstor.org/stable/40752982.

Ernst, Morris L., and David Loth. *American Sexual Behavior and the Kinsey Report.* New York: Greystone, 1948.

Everett, Bethany G., Kyl Myers, Jessica N. Sanders, and David K. Turok. "Male Abortion Beneficiaries: Exploring the Long-Term Educational and Economic Associations of Abortion among Men Who Report Teen Pregnancy." *Journal of Adolescent Health* 65, no. 4 (2019): 520–26. https://doi.org/10.1016/j.jadohealth.2019.05.001.

Fagan, Patrick F., and Aaron Churchill. *The Effect of Divorce on Children.* Marriage and Religion Research Institute (Washington, D.C.: 2012).

Falk, Armin, Anke Becker, Thomas Dohmen, David Huffman, and Uwe Sunde. "The Preference Survey Module: A Validated Instrument for Measuring Risk, Time, and Social Preferences." *Management Science* 69, no. 4 (2022): 1935–50. https://doi.org/10.1287/mnsc.2022.4455.

Fergusson, David M., Joseph M. Boden, and John Horwood. "Abortion among Young Women and Subsequent Life Outcomes." *Perspectives on Sexual and Reproductive Health* 39, no. 1 (Mar 2007): 6–12. https://doi.org/10.1363/3900607.

Folbre, Nancy. *Valuing Children: Rethinking the Economics of the Family.* Harvard University Press, 2008. doi:10.2307/j.ctvjnrt57.

Frederick, Shane, George Loewenstein, and Ted O'Donoghue. "Time Discounting and Time Preference: A Critical Review." *Journal of Economic Literature* 40, no. 2 (2002): 351–401. https://doi.org/10.1257/002205102320161311.

Freeman, Derek. *Margaret Mead and Samoa: The Making and Unmaking of an Anthropological Myth.* Cambridge, MA: Harvard University Press, 1983.

Freud, Sigmund. "'Civilized' Sexual Morality and Modern Nervous Illness." The Standard Edition of the Complete Psychological Works of Sigmund Freud, Volume IX (1906–1908). (1908 (2017)).

———. *A General Introduction to Psychoanalysis*. New York: Permabook Edition, 1953.

Gebhard, Paul H., Wardell B. Pomeroy, Clyde E. Martin, and Cornelia V. Christenson. *Pregnancy, Birth and Abortion*. New York: Harper & Brothers, and Paul B. Hoeber 1958.

Gissler, Mika, Elina Karalis, and Veli-Matti Ulander. "Decreased Suicide Rate after Induced Abortion, after the Current Care Guidelines in Finland 1987–2012." *Scandinavian Journal of Public Health* 43, no. 1 (2015): 99–101. https://doi.org/10.1177/1403494814560844.

Gold, Malcolm C. Divorce and Divorce Reform: A Reconciliation of Results at Odds. 2010. Working Paper. University of Wisconsin Marshfield/Wood County, Marshfield, WI.

Grant, George. *Grand Illusions: The Legacy of Planned Parenthood*. 2nd Edition ed. Franklin, TN: Adroit, 1992.

Green, Richard. "John Money, Ph.D. (July 8, 1921–July 7, 2006): A Personal Obituary." *Archives of Sexual Behavior* 35, no. 6 (2006): 629–32. https://doi.org/10.1007/s10508-006-9132-5.

Gruden, Wayne, and Barry Asmus. *The Poverty of Nations: A Sustainable Solution*. Wheaton, IL: Crossway, 2013.

Guiso, Luigi, Paola Sapienza, and Luigi Zingales. "Does Culture Affect Economic Outcomes?." *The Journal of Economic Perspectives* 20, no. 2 (2006): 23–48. http://www.jstor.org/stable/30033649.

Hajnal, J. "European Marriage Patterns in Perspective." In *Population in History: Essays in Historical Demography*, edited by D.V. Glass and D.E.C. Eversley, 101–43. London: Edward Arnold, 1965.

Hayek, F. A. *Law, Legislation and Liberty, Volume 1 : Rules and Order*. Chicago, IL: University of Chicago Press, 1973.

Hazlitt, Henry. *The Failure of the "New Economics": An Analysis of the Keynesian Fallacies*. Princeton, NJ: D. Van Nostrand Company, Inc., 1959.

Henrich, Joseph Patrick. *The Weirdest People in the World: How the West Became Psychologically Peculiar and Particularly Prosperous*. New York: Farrar, Straus and Giroux, 2020.

Hoppe, Hans-Hermann. *Democracy the God That Failed: The Economics and Politics of Monarcy, Democracy, and Natural Order*. New Brunswick: Transaction 2001.

Horack, Frank E. "Sex Offenses and Scientific Investigation." *Illinois Law Review* 44 (1949): 149–59.

Hough, Richard. *Captain Bligh and Mr Christian: The Men and the Mutiny*. New York: E. P. Dutton & Co., 1973.

Hull, N.E.H., and Peter Charles Hoffer. *Roe V. Wade: The Abortion Rights Controversy in American History*. Lawrence: University Press of Kansas, 2001.

Hurtado, Larry W. *Destroyer of the Gods: Early Christian Distinctiveness in the Roman World*. Waco, TX: Baylor University Press, 2017.

Huxley, Aldous. *Brave New World*. 1st electronic ed. New York: Rosetta LLC, 2000. https://research.ebsco.com/linkprocessor/plink?id=15524852-a2de-3c49-81a1-d73565227852.

Ikeda, Shinsuke. *The Economics of Self-Destructive Choices*. Tokyo: Springer, 2016.

Jeffrey, Linda, and Ronald D. Ray. *A History of the American Law Institute's Model Penal Code: The Kinsey Report' Influence on "Science-Based" Legal Reform 1923-2007*. First Principles, Inc. (2007).

Jeglic, Elizabeth. "The Long-Lasting Consequences of Child Sexual Abuse." *Psychology Today*, 2021.

Jones, E. Michael. *Degenerate Moderns: Modernity as Rationalized Sexual Misbehavior*. South Bend, IN: Fidelity, 2012.

———. *Libido Dominandi: Sexual Liberation and Political Control*. South Bend, IN: Fidelity, 2000.

Jordan, James B. *Part 2: From Children to Adults*. Audio file. Reading the Bible (Again) for the First Time 2009 (?).

———. *Part 3: The Bible Is a Story*. Audio file. Reading the Bible (Again) for the First Time 2009 (?).

———. *Primeval Saints*. Moscow, ID: Canon, 2001.

Kearney, Melissa S. *The Two-Parent Privilege: How Americans Stopped Getting Married and Started Falling Behind*. Chicago: The University of Chicago Press, 2023.

Keynes, John Maynard. *The Economic Consequences of the Peace*. New York: Harcourt, Brace and Howe, 1920.

———. *Economic Possibilities for Our Grandchildren*. New York: W.W. Norton & Co., 1930 (1963).

———. *The General Theory of Employment, Interest, and Money*. The University of Adelaide Library: Electronic Texts Collection, 1936.

———. *A Tract on Monetary Reform*. London: MacMillan and Co., Limited, 1923.

———. *Two Memoirs*. London: Rubert Hart-Davis, 1949.

Kinsey, Alfred C., Wardell B. Pomeroy, and Clyde E. Martin. *Sexual Behavior in the Human Male*. W.B. Saunders Co., 1948.

Kinsey, Alfred C., Wardell B. Pomeroy, Clyde E. Martin, and Paul H. Gebhard. *Sexual Behavior in the Human Female*. Saunders, 1953.

Klick, J., and T. Stratmann. "The Effect of Abortion Legalization on Sexual Behavior: Evidence from Sexually Transmitted Diseases." *Journal of Legal Studies* 32, no. 2 (2003): 407-33. https://doi.org/10.1086/377049.

Koyama, Mark, and Jared Rubin. *How the World Became Rich: The Historical Origins of Economic Growth*. Cambridge, UK: Polity, 2022.

Kuh, Richard H. "A Prosecutor Considers the Model Penal Code." *Columbia Law Review* 63, no. 4 (1963): 608-31. https://doi.org/10.2307/1120579.

Kuran, Timur. *Private Truths, Public Lies: The Social Consequences of Preference Falsification*. Cambridge, Mass.: Harvard University Press, 1995.

———. "The Scale of Entrepreneurship in Middle Eastern History: Inhibitive Roles of Islamic Institutions." In *The Invention of Enterprise:*

BIBLIOGRAPHY

Entrepreneurship from Ancient Mesopotamia to Modern Times, edited by David S. Mokyr Landes, Joel Baumol, William J., 62–87. Princeton, NJ: Princeton University Press, 2012.

———. "Why the Middle East Is Economically Underdeveloped: Historical Mechanisms of Institutional Stagnation." *Journal of Economic Perspectives* 18, no. 3 (2004): 71–90. https://doi.org/10.1257/0895330042162421.

La Porta, Rafael, Florencio Lopez-de-Silanes, Andrei Shleifer, and Robert w Vishny. "Law and Finance." *Journal of Political Economy* 106, no. 6 (1998): 1113–55. https://doi.org/10.1086/250042.

Landes, David S. *Revolution in Time: Clocks and the Making of the Modern World*. Cambridge, MA: The Belknap Press, 1983.

———. *The Wealth and Poverty of Nations: Why Some Are So Rich and Some So Poor*. New York: W.W. Norton & Company, Inc., 1999.

Lipset, Seymour Martin. "The Work Ethic, Then and Now." *Journal of Labor Research* 13, no. 1 (1992): 45–54. https://doi.org/10.1007/BF02685449.

Logan, Wayne, Lindsay S. Stellwagen, and Patrick A. Langan. *Felony Laws of the 50 States and the District of Columbia, 1986*. U.S. Department of Justice Bureau of Justice Statistics (1987).

Lowrey, Annie. "The Most Important Study in the Abortion Debate." *The Atlantic*, 2022.

Luke, George, "John Money, David Reimer, and the Dark Origins of the Transgender Movement," 2019.

Lummis, Trevor. *Pitcairn Island: Life and Death in Eden*. Hants, England: Ashgate, 1997.

Malinowski, Bronislaw. *The Sexual Life of Savages in North-Western Melanesia; an Ethnographic Account of Courtship, Marriage, and Family Life among the Natives of the Trobriand Islands, British New Guinea*. Harvest Book. New York: Harcourt, Brace & World, 1929.

Malthus, Thomas R. *An Essay on the Principle of Population*. London: J. Johnson, 1798.

Mangalwadi, Vishal. "Sex: The Secret of the West's Economic Success." no. March 27, 2023. (2017). https://affluentinvestor.com/2017/09/sex-secret-wests-economic-success/.

Marina, William F. "Egalitarianism and Empire." *Studies in History and Philosophy*, no. August 2, 2024. (1975).

Marinov, Bojidar. "Civilization and Self-Control." *AmericanVision.org*, 2010.

———. "A Tale of Two Islands." *AmericanVision.org*, 2011.

McCleary, Rachel M., and Robert J. Barro. "Protestants and Catholics and Educational Investment in Guatemala." In *Advances in the Economics of Religion*, edited by Jean-Paul Carvalho, Sriya Iyer and Jared Rubin, 169–95. Cham: Springer International 2019.

McCloskey, Deirdre Nansen, and Art Carden. *Leave Me Alone and I'll Make You Rich: How the Bourgeois Deal Enriched the World*. Chicago: The University of Chicago Press, 2020.

McCord, Gordon C., and Jeffrey D. Sachs. "Physical Geography and the History of Economic Development." *Faith & Economics* 66 (2015): 11–43.

Mead, Margaret. *Coming of Age in Samoa: A Psychological Study of Primitive Youth for Western Civilization.* New York: William Morrow & Company, 1928.

Media, RightNow. *Leader's Guide, Session 4: Titus 2:1–10.*

Mischel, Walter, Yuichi Shoda, and Monica L. Rodriguez. "Delay of Gratification in Children." *Science* 244, no. 4907 (1989): 933–38. http://www.jstor.org/stable/1704494.

Mobilewalla. *New Report Reveals Demographics of Black Lives Matter Protesters Shows Vast Majority Are White, Marched within Their Own Cities.* (www.prnewswire.com: 2020). https://www.prnewswire.com/news-releases/new-report-reveals-demographics-of-black-lives-matter-protesters-shows-vast-majority-are-white-marched-within-their-own-cities-301079234.html.

Mohr, James C. *Abortion in America: The Origins and Evolution of National Policy, 1800–1900.* New York: Oxford University Press, 1978.

Mokyr, Joel. "False Dichotomy." *Liberty Matters*, 2014.

Mølland, Eirin. "Benefits from Delay? The Effect of Abortion Availability on Young Women and Their Children." *Labour Economics* 43 (2016): 6–28. https://doi.org/https://doi.org/10.1016/j.labeco.2016.06.011.

Mota, Natalie P., Margaret Burnett, and Jitender Sareen. "Associations between Abortion, Mental Disorders, and Suicidal Behaviour in a Nationally Representative Sample." *Canadian Journal of Psychiatry* 55, no. 4 (2010): 239–47.

Mulligan, Robert F. "Religion as Adaptation: The Role of Time Preference ". In *Political Economy Research Focus*, edited by Walter R. Levin, 69–92. New York: Nova Science 2008.

Murray, Melissa. "Strange Bedfellows: Criminal Law, Family Law and the Legal Construction of Intimate Life." *Iowa Law Review* 94 (2009): 1253–313.

Newsmax. "Idaho's Gay Marriage Ban Remains in State Constitution." *www.newsmax.com.* (2015).

North, Douglass C. "Institutions." *Journal of Economic Perspectives* 5, no. 1 (1991): 97–112. https://doi.org/10.1257/jep.5.1.97.

———. *Structure and Change in Economic History.* New York: W.W. Norton & Company, 1981.

North, Gary. *Victim's Rights: The Biblical View of Civil Justice.* Tyler, TX: Institute for Christian Economics, 1990.

Olasky, Marvin. *Abortion Rites: A Social History of Abortion in America.* Washington D.C.: Regnery 1995.

Olasky, Marvin N. *The Press and Abortion 1938–1988.* Hillsdale, NJ: Lawrence Erlbaum Associates, 1988.

Parrinder, Geoffrey. *Sexual Morality in the World's Religions.* Oxford, England: Oneworld Publications, 1996.

BIBLIOGRAPHY

Pascoe, Peggy. *What Comes Naturally: Miscegenation Law and the Making of Race in America*. New York: Oxford University Press, 2009.

"Pedophilia, Exhibitionism, and Voyeurism: Legal Problems in the Deviant Society." *Georgia Law Review* 4, no. 1 (1969): 149–63.

Peters, Jan, and Christian Büchel. "The Neural Mechanisms of Inter-Temporal Decision-Making: Understanding Variability." *Trends in Cognitive Sciences* 15, no. 5 (2011): 227–39. https://doi.org/10.1016/j.tics.2011.03.002.

Piano, Clara E. "Autocratic Family Policy." *Constitutional Political Economy* 33, no. 2 (2022): 233–53. https://doi.org/10.1007/s10602-021-09356-4.

Podgor, Ellen S., Peter J. Henning, and Neil P. Cohen. *Mastering Criminal Law*. Durham, NC: Carolina Academic Press, 2008.

Posner, Richard A. "Social Norms and the Law; an Economic Approach." *The American Economic Review* 87, no. 2 (1997): 365–69.

Pritchard, A.C., and Todd J. Zywicki. "Finding the Constitution: An Economic Analysis of Tradition's Role in Constitutional Interpretation." *North Carolina Law Review* 77 (1998–1999): 409–522.

The Probation Response to Child Sexual Abuse Offenders: How Is It Working? . American Bar Association (Chicago, IL: 1990).

Rachewiltz, Boris de. *Black Eros : Sexual Customs of Africa from Prehistory to the Present Day*. London: George Allen & Unwin, 1964.

Reisman, Judith A. *Kinsey: Crimes & Consequences*. fourth ed. Arlington, VA: Institute for Media Education, 2012.

———. *Sexual Sabotage*. New York, NY: WND, 2010.

Reisman, Judith A., and Edward W. Eichel. *Kinsey, Sex and Fraud: The Indoctrination of a People*. Lafayette: Huntington House 1990.

———. *Kinsey, Sex and Fraud: The Indoctrination of a People*. Edited by J. Gordon Muir and John H. Court. Lafayette: Huntington House 1990.

Reisman, Judith A., and Mary E. Mcalister. "Nearly 60 Years after His Death, Alfred Kinsey's Pansexual Worldview Takes Root in Marriage Decisions." *Journal on Gender, Race, and Justice* VI, no. II (2016): 25–55.

Richardson, Gary. "Craft Guilds and Christianity in Late-Medieval England:A Rational-Choice Analysis." *Rationality and Society* 17, no. 2 (2005): 139–89. https://doi.org/10.1177/1043463105051631.

Robinson, Paul, and Markus Dubber. "The American Model Penal Code: A Brief Overview." *New Criminal Law Review* 10 (2007).

Rose, David C. *The Moral Foundations of Economic Behavior*. New York, NY: Oxford University Press, 2011.

Rupasingha, Anil, Stephan J. Goetz, and David Freshwater. "The Production of Social Capital in U.S. Counties.." *Journal of Socio-Economics* 35 (2006): 83–101.

Rushdoony, Rousas J. *The Institutes of Biblical Law*. Phillipsburg, NJ: Presbyterian and Reformed 1973.

———. *Politics of Guilt and Pity*. Vallecito, CA: Ross House, 1995.

———. *Systematic Theology in Two Volumes*. 2 vols. Vol. 2, Vallecito, CA: Ross House 1994.

BIBLIOGRAPHY

Sauer, R. "Attitudes to Abortion in America, 1800–1973." *Population Studies* 28, no. 1 (1974): 53–67.

Schoeck, Helmut. *Envy: A Theory of Social Behavior.* Indianapolis: Liberty Fund, 1966.

Schultz, Chris, "The Tamarisk Tree," *The Well Blog*, October 29, 2015.

Shah, Rebecca Samuel. "Religion and Economic Empowerment among the Enterprising Poor." *The Review of Faith & International Affairs* 11, no. 4 (2013): 41–45. https://doi.org/10.1080/15570274.2013.857121.

Shakeshaft, Charol. *Educator Sexual Misconduct: A Synthesis of Existing Literature.* Washington, D.C., 2004.

Shavell, Steven. "Law Versus Morality as Regulators of Conduct." *American Law and Economics Review* 4 (2002): 227–57.

Siecus Report. (New York: Sexuality Information and Education Council of the United States, 1996).

Slovenko, Ralph, and Cyril Phillips. "Psychosexuality and the Criminal Law." *Vanderbilt Law Review* 15 (1962): 797–828.

Smith, Adam. *Wealth of Nations.* Electric Book Company, 2000, 1776.

Smith, T. Alexander. *Time and Public Policy.* Knoxville: The University of Tennessee Press, 1988.

Smock, Erica. *What If Roe Fell? The State-by-State Consequences of Overturning Roe V. Wade.* Center for Reproductive Rights (New York: 2004).

Sorokin, Pitirim A. *Sane Sex Order.* Bombay: Bharatiya Vidya Bhavan, 1961.

Stanley, Scott M., and Galena K. Rhoades. *What's the Plan? Cohabitation, Engagement, and Divorce.* Institute for Family Studies (Charlottesville, VA: 2023).

Stark, Rodney. *The Victory of Reason: How Christianity Led to Freedom, Capitalism, and Western Success.* New York: Random House, 2005.

Stark, Rodney, and Roger Finke. *Acts of Faith: Explaining the Human Side of Religion.* Berkeley: Univeristy of California Press, 2000.

Steingrimsdottir, Herdis. "Reproductive Rights and the Career Plans of U.S. College Freshmen." *Labour Economics* 43 (2016): 29–41. https://doi.org/10.1016/j.labeco.2016.07.001.

Sunde, Uwe, Thomas Dohmen, Benjamin Enke, Armin Falk, David Huffman, and Gerrit Meyerheim. "Patience and Comparative Development." *The Review of Economic Studies* 89, no. 5 (2021): 2806–40. https://doi.org/10.1093/restud/rdab084.

Surkheel, Abu Aaliyah. "The Male Lust, the Female Form and the Forbidden Gaze." *The Muslim Marriage Guide*, 2019.

Thompson, E. P. "Time, Work-Discipline, and Industrial Capitalism." *Past & Present* 38, no. 1 (1967): 56–97. https://doi.org/10.1093/past/38.1.56.

Tilgher, Adriano. *Work: What It Has Meant to Men through the Ages (Homo Faber).* Translated by Dorothy Canfield Fisher. New York: Harcourt Brace, 1930.

Torcia, Charles E. *Wharton's Criminal Law 15th Edition.* Vol. 1, New York: Clark Boardman Callaghan, 1993.

Unwin, Joseph D. *Hopousia or the Sexual and Economic Foundations of a New Society*. New York: Oskar Piest, 1940.

———. "Monogamy as a Condition of Social Energy." *The Hibbert Journal* XXV, no. 4 (1927): 662-77.

———. *Sex and Culture*. London: Oxford University Press, 1934.

———. *Sexual Regulations and Cultural Behaviour*. London: Oxford University Press, 1935.

Waite, Linda J., and Maggie Gallagher. *The Case for Marriage: Why Married People Are Happier, Healthier, and Better Off Financially*. New York: Doubleday, 2000.

Walker, Timothy. *Introduction to American Law : Designed as a First Book for Students*. 1st Edition ed. Philadelphia: P.H. Nicklin & T. Johnson, Law Booksellers, 1837.

Wardle, Lynn D. "The "Withering Away" of Marriage: Some Lessons from the Bolshevik Family Law Reforms in Russia, 1917-1926." *Georgetown Journal of Law & Public Policy* 2, no. 2 (2004): 469-522.

Weber, Max. *The Protestant Ethic and the Spirit of Capitalism*. Translated by Talcott Parsons. Charles Scribner's Sons, 1930 (1905).

Wharton, John Jane Smith. *An Exposition of the Laws Relating to the Women of England : Showing Their Rights, Remedies, and Responsibilities in Every Position of Life*. London: E. Spettigue, Printer, 1853.

Whittler, Charles H. *Abortions in World Religions*. Congressional Research Service: The Library of Congress (Washington, D. C.: 1988).

Wie, Jeong Ha, Su Kyung Nam, Hyun Sun Ko, Jong Chul Shin, In Yang Park, and Young Lee. "The Association between Abortion Experience and Postmenopausal Suicidal Ideation and Mental Health: Results from the 5th Korean National Health and Nutrition Examination Survey (Knhanes V)." *Taiwanese Journal of Obstetrics and Gynecology* 58, no. 1 (2019): 153-58. https://doi.org/10.1016/j.tjog.2018.11.028.

Wilson, Margo, and Martin Daly. "Do Pretty Women Inspire Men to Discount the Future?." *Proceedings of the Royal Society of London. Series B: Biological Sciences* 271, no. Suppl 4 (2004): S177-S79. https://doi.org/10.1098/rsbl.2003.0134.

Witte, John. *From Sacrament to Contract: Marriage, Religion, and Law in the Western Tradition, Family, Religion, and Culture*. Louisville, KY: Westminster John Knox, 1997.

Woodberry, Robert D. "The Missionary Roots of Liberal Democracy." *American Political Science Review* 106, no. 2 (2012): 244-74. https://doi.org/10.1017/S0003055412000093.

Wright, John Paul, Kevin M. Beaver, Mark Alden Morgan, and Eric J. Connolly. "Political Ideology Predicts Involvement in Crime." *Personality and Individual Differences* 106 (2017): 236-41. https://doi.org/10.1016/j.paid.2016.10.062.

BIBLIOGRAPHY

Yancey, Philip. "The Lost Sex Study: If We Make a God of Sexuality, That God Will Fail in Ways That Affect the Whole Person and Perhaps the Whole Society." *Christianity Today*, 1994.

Zabin, Laurie S., Marilyn B. Hirsch, and Mark R. Emerson. "When Urban Adolescents Choose Abortion: Effects on Education, Psychological Status and Subsequent Pregnancy." *Family Planning Perspectives* 21, no. 6 (1989): 248–55.

www.ingramcontent.com/pod-product-compliance
Lightning Source LLC
Chambersburg PA
CBHW072130160426
43197CB00012B/2058